G000152324

BEHIND THE SMILE

You'll never know what a smile can hide.

Table of Contents

Foreword

This story is not intended to evoke sympathy, rather provide strength and courage. Whilst our circumstances may shape us, Behind the Smile shows that they do not have to be what ultimately defines us.

Paulette's compelling narrative tells her story from early childhood, through to adulthood factually accounting events as she remembers them. The second layer of the book is a deeper journey into painful memories and difficult periods, again there is no desire to evoke pity, but only to show the magnitude of grace and healing that is present in Paulette's life.

Mental health and domestic violence are themes that have, for too long, held a stigma and been taboo subjects. This culture of silence, effectively holds people captive in vicious cycles of aggression and depression. It could happen to anyone, and it is imperative that we have an open dialogue that leaves no place for guilt and shame to permeate the victim.

Paulette's story is that of strength and courage that she bravely shares with us as a testimony of God's transformative power in her life and it is her deepest desire that you too may feel the impact of the love and grace of God through the pages of this book.

Pastor Amanda Dye, Kensington Temple LCC.

Preface

This book is not just a story, it is a testimony of how God used a broken girl to tell of strength, grace and mercy.

"The purpose of a testimony isn't just to tell the testimony; the testimony is supposed to empower the listener to also overcome in their life" - *Andrew Anyanwu, Children and Youth Pastor at Kensington Temple* LCC.

You will read stories from my childhood into recent adult life and most importantly an aspect I consider the turning point in my life. Being honest, I never thought that my story was worth telling but having shared some aspects of it with a few people who know me, not as a mechanism for sympathy but as an experience to foster love and strength in them, a resounding theme was for me to share this publicly.

It is in this vein that during 2018, God really used the season for me to share my story even more and on a few occasions to an audience of strangers. I felt empowered by the positive responses I got and was encouraged to start writing a blog. Soon after starting the blog, the feedback was amazing but then I realised that people wanted to know more and I could not keep up with the blog due to time and family demand. I decided it a better option to tell it all in a book to empower and help others who may be going through the same or similar situations.

In the first few paragraphs of this book, you would note, as much as I avoid the use of would, should and could, there is a proliferation of these. This is to make a point. My hope is you get it.

To be candid, like you, there are things from my past I would rather forget. Yet there is no power in forgetting. It was hard for me to go back over what I have been through whether in my childhood, teenage years or the beginning of my adulthood but it had to be done for the purpose of this book. In writing this book, I was able to break free from all the negative feelings of those experiences and see the many lessons behind every smile and every tear. You would be surprised I can have belly roaring laughter now; a sure sign of redemptive and restorative healing. I pray this book will have the impact intended and that many lives will be transformed by it.

The power in my story may be the very thing that brings your life through to the love of Jesus Christ. I pray it speaks to people everywhere - children, teenagers, young adults and mature women/men. I pray you would know that you are loved and made for a purpose.

To me, this is more than just a book, this is a powerful testimony to the glory of God and I hope you will also share the same feeling by the end of it. I believe you will enjoy reading this book as I have put it all in there though condensed to fit in but the important bits are all there. I don't think people realise how much strength it takes to pull yourself out of a dark place mentally.

Paulette Monteiro, Author.

Chapter 1
Where it all began

I was born in 1983 in Toulouse, South of France. I was born prematurely. I was born with a hip alignment problem called DDH[1],which doctors thought would make it difficult for me to walk properly. Well, I guess they were wrong because I walked when I was 9 months though my dad recalls my walk being "funny" but I'm walking perfectly now.

I am the second eldest on my mum's side and the firstborn of my dad. I have 6 sisters and 2 brothers, I don't do "halves" or anything else, we are all brothers and sisters as far as I am concerned.

To the best of my knowledge, my mum and dad would have been 21 and 24 respectively when they had me. My dad recalls how happy they were when they found out my mum was pregnant with me - a prayer answered. My older sister was nearly 2 years old then. I wonder how she felt about having a little sister. I don't believe she would remember herself.

It still amazes me how certain parents select their children's names; Paulette is such an old French name, in my opinion mostly reserved for old ladies. I have never met a "Paulette" my age,

---

[1] Developmental dysplasia of the hip (DDH) is a problem with the way a baby's hip joint forms. Sometimes the condition starts before the baby is born, and sometimes it happens after birth, as the child grows. It can affect one hip or both. Most infants treated for DDH develop into active, healthy kids and have no hip problems.

ever. I was very unhappy about that name choice. My mum explained that I was named after the wonderful midwife who took care of her and me during our time at the hospital, which my dad also confirmed later on. Couldn't she have a better name? Though it was a nice thought, I wasn't impressed at all.

Throughout my teenage years, I was known and introduced myself as "Paula". As a child, I remember being teased a lot because of that name, nothing too horrible i.e. "Paulette, omelette". Boys would chant this in the playground which would drive me insane. I hated that name with a passion. Note that nowadays, those who call me "Paula" would have probably known me for a very long time. As I grew older, my name started to grow on me. I like it now as I can see its uniqueness, it is certainly not a common name.

Childhood memories
My earliest childhood memories are from the age of 5; everything before then seems blank. I have absolutely no memories of my dad or the life we had before. So let me tell you what I remember! My first memory is when we arrived in Kinshasa, Democratic Republic of Congo, that's my first memory. I certainly don't remember getting on the plane and if it was my first time on a plane surely I should remember that, right!? But I don't.

Anyway, arriving in a "strange" country was only the beginning of 'life' for me. My mum, who would have been about 26 years old at the time, left my sister and me in my grandmother's care. From what I was told, she had very little family support back in France hence her decision and I can safely assume she probably thought it would be better for us to grow up around family. For people reading this book and not familiar with African families, it is common practice, due to the cost of childcare in developed countries, for parents to send their wards/children back home to grandparents. I reckon it was difficult for her to be that young and solely bringing up two young children. I understand the struggle – I will tell you my own struggle a bit later in this book.

My mum was known to travel a lot due to her lifestyle hence she did not have a known base. She moved around quite a lot from what I have been told, therefore she did what she thought was best for her children. I believe it is a difficult decision for a mother to leave her children in the care of relatives in another country. A mother would always want and do what she thinks is best for her child as much as she knows-how; this I know is what my mother did.

At that time, my mum and dad were separated. A lot had happened from the moment they arrived from Angola to France. It's a long story of which I do not have all the details to share or form an informed opinion. Besides, my mum is not here to give an account.

I remember waving goodbye to my mum as she left in the taxi to go to the airport, I don't think we quite knew what was happening. Being so young, I think all that mattered was that I was with my sister; being together was a great comfort. Over the years that followed, she would visit us as often as she could.

Living with our grandmother was a big change for us, she lived in the village and we were city children and everything around us was very different. It took some time getting used to these new surroundings and the people. Aside from the major culture shock, we had no understanding of the local language, Lingala. We managed with French interspersed with a bit of Lingala – beyond that we had no comprehension! I would like to tell you it was strange yet funny when we tried to strike communication.

We were quickly introduced to the concept of family gatherings. Compared to our family France, our family in the Congo was very united. We would see relatives drop by on a regular basis and have activities including parties, ad hoc catch-ups, etc. – there was always a reason to gather as a family. It was very enjoyable to be in that kind of atmosphere. My big sister and I absolutely loved it.

As for school, I remember walking up a steep hill to get to the school, we wore uniforms and sang the national anthem at the hoisted the national flag every morning. The teachers were very strict and even had the right to beat you. I don't remember receiving any but surely did witness some of my classmates and other school children do. This wasn't something parents would go to the school and complain about, how strange! Back then, the games we played in and outside school were very simple i.e. telling a story from drawings on the sandy ground to creating a fashion show with colourful materials found in our homes. We didn't have any care in the world and it was great!

Chapter 2
From Childhood to Adulthood - The Lone Ranger

In the early 90s, our mum came back to visit us again but this time she was taking us back to France. I believe I was around 7 years old. We were sad to leave our family and friends behind yet were definitely happy to be reunited with our mum and at the thought of being with her every day.

Back in France, we lived in Paris for a short while and moved to Toulouse where most of our family were. I remember our mum still going back and forth to Congo. She made sure her sister, nephew and brother joined us in Toulouse when we had settled. Her heart was always in the right place and she helped a lot of people making their way to Europe, I will always remember that.

Foster care debut

I don't recall how my sister and I ended up in foster care, but one day we did. Most of our childhood, when we got back to France, was spent with our mum and in foster care with foster parents or in care homes. We were in foster care on and off for some years but I've always been with my sister. It is not usual practice to find children from the same family kept together. I consider us lucky. Thinking about foster care brings back both good and not-so-good memories.

Our mum was very present and involved though all I can remember is that we moved homes and locations a lot!

My childhood is nothing I believe I can brag about except I did enjoy amazing activities such as horse riding lessons, skiing trips in the winter, the drives to the beach in the summer and the numerous after school club activities. I knew most children my age did not do as much as we did. I know that is certainly more than what some would or could do but to me, those were not exceptional things. I guess I may have taken them for granted.

My family

As mentioned before, I have 6 sisters and 2 brothers. Yes, that is a lot but let me explain in order for you to understand the rest of my story. On my mum's side, I have 3 sisters and I am the second born. On my dad's side, I have 2 sisters and 2 brothers and I am his firstborn. I also have a sister who is my stepmum's niece whom they adopted as a child.

In 1991, during our last year in Toulouse, our little sister was born. She may have been 1 year old when we moved to Lille. In Lille, my big sister and I were back in foster care while our little sister lived with our mum in a small studio flat. I think the main reason why, at that time, we stayed in a care home was because our mum was not settled down but also because she could not afford a bigger flat to accommodate us all.

The cycle

From what you read, you can understand that our lives were pretty much set in an undefined and unwanted rhythm - foster home to foster family to mum and back into the same cycle. Whilst in foster care, mum always made the effort to visit, it never felt like she was an absent mother but she was still missing the important bits. I probably had all my major achievements while in foster care i.e learning to ride a bike. Don't get me wrong, I wish I was with my mum all the time but I somehow got used to it, I had desensitised myself to whatever emotions I could feel. I knew it was impossible and I learned to accept things just the way they were. To be honest, I did not mind. I know it sounds heartless but I was young and I learned to adapt.

My experience of being in the "system" wasn't that bad, except for one part which I will discuss in Chapter 4. Strange things have happened there but nothing out of the ordinary I guess. Being in that environment, I got to do a lot of things I wouldn't have done growing up in an African home hence in a way, I am grateful for the experience and the way this has opened up my mind to new things.

Whether in care homes or in foster families, my sister and I have always been together. As I mentioned in the previous chapter this was a comfort to both of us. I think it also brought comfort to our mum. I know we were blessed to be together when other siblings have been split apart whilst in the "system".

In France, it might be different elsewhere, care homes are places where children stay for a while when their parents cannot take care of them for various reasons. It may be for weeks, months or years. It's a big house with a lot of children and adults on a rota looking after us, day and night. The adults on-site managed the place and looked after us, especially the younger ones. We were all assigned a key worker and I will always remember ours, he was like a father figure to us. He taught me how to fish and ride a bike.

We had our meals together on big tables which we took in turns to set. Things were very structured from breakfast to showers to school to snack time etc. Pretty much everything was run on a schedule. Most of us were encouraged to take part in activities on Wednesday afternoons as there was no school. the activities could be anything you like, I often wondered where the money came from because we were all doing something. I believe I made the most of that by joining Karate, Boxing, Kickboxing and many more. Weekends were always packed with fun outdoor activities which we enjoyed when we were not spending them with our mum. Compared to our peers at school, we were definitely privileged. Most children in the care home received visits from their parents, if not every weekend for the lucky ones, at least every 2 weeks but for the less fortunate (as I would call them), it was on a monthly basis or none.

From my experience, I am well aware that not all care homes are the same.

Detached
Having moved around quite a lot as a child, I never made lasting friendships. That's one thing I always regretted; I moved schools so often there was never an opportunity to. It, however, has a rather advantageous aspect; my focus was more on my studies than on making friends. The thought of the heartbreak of leaving friends behind made it slightly easier for me to not get attached. I was detached emotionally but still envious of finding people who had been friends since Nursery. I longed to settle in one place and have friends with whom I could recall our past years in school as in "Do you remember last year...". Having these sorts of friendships meant that I belonged somewhere and was part of something.

If you are reading the book and have gotten this far, I would encourage you to speak to a leader of your church or cell group about similar things. Healthy human relationships are essential for physical, spiritual and emotional growth and quite important that you heal from past hurts and emotional detachments as I call it. I now realise that, through the culmination of past pain and other issues, I had built a wall around my heart and kept people at a distance.

This went on until I was about 9 or 10 years old when we got settled in a foster home in Lille, North of France. That foster home was the same one we previously lived in. Our mum lived with our sister. My big sister and I stayed in the same care home for 3 consecutive years only seeing our mum some weekends, this was not regular. I never actually stopped to think what our mum was doing during the times we were in care, I just got on with things. I think I didn't want to get attached to anyone, even her, emotionally. I was only attached and cared mostly about my sister. She seemed happy to see us during those weekends and we were happy to be with her - an effective unspoken arrangement.

We had no family in Lille and our mum was a full-time mum who eventually got involved with the wrong people. She was arrested and sentenced to serve a couple of months in prison. From then on, our little sisters entered the care system. It was still a shock to us.

My little sister, the one directly after me, had been in care previously in Lille when she was very young, she must have been 3 years old. I remember going to visit her with our social worker. When it was time to leave, she screamed and cried so much, my heart was in pieces. I cried all the way back. I mean, my big sister and I were used to being in care but it was her first experience and because she was much younger than us she could not be where we were at that time. Her cries haunted me for a couple of days. She wanted to be with us and we wanted to be with her too. After going through this, I vowed to never let anything like that happen to my children.

A couple of months later, my aunt came from Toulouse and took my younger sister out of foster care to go live with her. I think she was granted temporary custody at the time. She visited us in our foster home to give us the news and for us to say goodbye to our sister. Our mum was aware of everything that was happening and would write to us as often as she could to reassure us.

When our mum was released, she went to Belgium to live with her partner at the time. A couple of months later, she gave birth to our youngest sister. This was a surprise to us, especially since we were not aware that she was expecting and deducted that she went to prison being pregnant. We received pictures of our baby sister while in foster care and were very excited. She was born prematurely and had to be incubated for several months so our mum wasn't able to leave Belgium to visit us. When our little sister came out of the hospital, our mum moved back to Toulouse to join our little sister who was with our aunt and settled there. We couldn't wait to see the latest addition to our family.

Because we hadn't seen our mum for a long time, on a particular Christmas holiday, I remember vividly, our social worker driving us from Lille to Toulouse so we could spend Christmas with our mother and sisters. That was a long journey! Let me take this opportunity to applaud the good and caring social workers we were blessed with; this was one of them. Later on, our mum, with the help of our assigned social worker, started the process for us to be reunited in the same city at least. Shortly after filing the paperwork and consulting with the children's court, we were transferred from our care home in Lille to another care home in Toulouse. Once again we found ourselves packing our lives in small suitcases though this time we embarked on a plane journey by ourselves only supervised by the air hostesses. Being in Toulouse meant that we had the opportunity to be out most weekends and spend time with our extended family more frequently.

I think that was a good move for us however, I wished we were at home with our mum and sisters.

We thought it would only be a matter of time before we could be reunited properly but our mum got really sick and the girls were placed together in a foster family until she got better. Though she never really got better, she was able to look after the sister who comes after me and the last born stayed with the foster family and regularly visited with occasional stays.

A sense of belonging

In that season, I noted I had a new sense of happiness yet there was a nagging need within me. I will try and describe it as much as I can – I believe that in every family there is at least one person who feels like they do not fit in. Well, in my family, I felt it was me and convinced it had been the case throughout my childhood and teenage years.

I never really felt I belonged anywhere growing up, not even in my own family. I was the odd girl. My features are just not what you'd see in my immediate family, I am short and my skin colour is a shade darker. My love for school, books, and studies, in general, is definitely not something you'll find in my immediate family. I also grew up in locations where most often than not, I was the only black girl in my class (we could at times be 3 or 4 in the entire school).

At school, I was that student who would remind the teacher about homework, get excited about tests/unplanned tests and even ask for extra homework. That is how much I loved school. My thirst for knowledge was something quite bizarre to most people around me, I always wanted to know more and more. Also, I didn't like school holidays at all! I felt it was a waste of time but I made the most of it by diving into books and of course, my assignments were always done before the holiday started. That is how much of a nerd I was.

The overachiever in me
You could say that I was an overachiever and I was okay with it, it was the only time I felt I mattered and I was good at something. Teachers were always so proud of my work and achievements. Yes, this is a confession, as much as I was emotionally detached from anyone, I used to thrive on the praises of my teachers.

I even skipped a class! Yes, I did 1 term of CM1 (Year 5 equivalent) and because of my high test scores, I should really say perfect grades in all the subjects, I was told I should be moved to CM2 (Year 6 equivalent). My test scores were way above what was expected from that year group. I continually obtained the highest scores in all my tests. Following a meeting between my class teacher and the headteacher, the headteacher called a meeting with my foster home key worker and my mum, to discuss my outstanding work and a possible direct move to CM2. They were very excited but I was very worried to find myself with older children and a new teacher. To make this move as easy as possible, we agreed on a trial period. The classwork in CM2 was more challenging and I enjoyed it so I stayed. Since that time, I had always been the youngest in my class. Although I was excelling in school, I never shook the feeling of always being the odd one out. It reared its head at this stage of my life again. Yes, this was a great thing but in CM2 I didn't feel like I belonged with the big boys and girls just yet as I had to leave my classmates behind.

I would like to point out here that back then one of my love languages[2] was "Words of Affirmation", I no longer live for the praise of Men, as I did for the praise of my teachers when I was in school. It helps you understand why my teachers' compliments and praise reports meant a lot to me.

Family life
At "home", I was quite boisterous and argued quite a lot with my sister and anyone who dared argue with me. I was mouthy but also very sarcastic I must admit. As we grew older, I started feeling detached from my sister too. Though I liked having her around I felt very different from her in every way. I didn't have the same interests as her or my female cousins, so I often felt left out. I was very envious of their relationship but I couldn't quite relate to them in any way – interests, books, etc.

I really felt misunderstood and wondered if I was in the right family to start with. "Maybe I was switched at birth", I wondered at times. I watched a movie once and I automatically related to the main character who was switched at birth. My imagination went wild.

I know you may be reading this and be familiar with that feeling too. Others may read this and wonder what I mean. Now I know that most times

---

[2] Check out Gary Chapman's Love Languages.

we do not fit in because we are called for a cause greater than what we know. Other times it is because of our own insecurities, behaviour, and attitude. If you are feeling that way most of the time, please be honest with yourself and open with those around you. No one should feel like they don't belong to the point of wanting to disappear.

My sister and female cousins would often leave me out in conversations and their fun activities in and outside the home. I lived in my own little bubble and at times pretended I was adopted. I used to dream my "real parents" were out there on big adventures, writing books and making new discoveries of archaeological sites around the world. Yes, I had high hopes that my love for archaeology had been passed down from my "real parents", and my dad was the next Indiana Jones. Again another confession - I dreamt a lot to escape the harsh realities of what I was going through at the time, I wonder how much money I would have made if I wrote a book from those 'day-dreams'.

My mum also found it hard to deal with me at times because I was very outspoken with a lot of attitudes (that was only at home, not at school) nothing like my darling big sister, who was not so perfect but more quiet, popular and liked by all. I also envied the relationship my mum and my sister had, it was somehow more natural than the one we had. I felt she favoured my sister over me. I was hurt at times by their display of affection and I may have hurt my mum too by refusing to be affectionate. I kept her at a safe distance and struggled to believe she really loved me. I couldn't help it, I felt like a misfit most of the time around my mum and my big sister. I never felt like I was wanted.

It was a challenge to relate to any member of my family – as hard as I tried, I could not make it work. I was me but then again I wished I was someone else most of the time. I was trying to live the life I was not born to live or living a life I knew I had to live but was not afforded to me. If only I knew then what God had said about me and His thoughts for me.

I wished for so many things that never came to pass.

People found my behaviour odd as I would often go from the fun girl to the "I-do-not- feel-like-talking" girl, I couldn't even explain what was going on within me, all I knew was that I didn't feel like I belonged anywhere. My childhood living arrangements didn't help that feeling and if anything it just made it worse. I felt unsettled emotionally and mentally which probably reflected on my behaviour. My mood could change very quickly.

You must be wondering why there has been no other mention of or reference to my dad. I really do not recall our time with him. I met him when I was 13 years old, which for me was the "first time". I have absolutely no memories of him before that time except a few instances when I would receive letters, money, and gifts from him. I never heard my mum say a bad word about my dad and I never asked her questions about him. He seemed like a nice man from what I could read and he seemed to genuinely care about me. Maybe my mum found it hard to love me because I reminded her of him. Those were my own feelings.

Depression
Looking back, I think I may have suffered from depression. Yes, children do and can suffer from depression. There was an uneasy feeling within

me. That feeling that makes you feel alone even when you have "millions" of people around you. I constantly felt rejected. I often felt like disappearing, "Who would miss me?" I thought to myself and each time my answer would be "No one". Deep down in my little soul, I was extremely sad.

I could be happy one second and quickly sink into a very dark place the next where my thoughts and issues would take over my whole being. My head felt like it was going to explode. I think I previously always struggled with unhelpful thinking patterns.

To make matters worse, in my early teenage years, I suddenly became body-conscious. I desired to find some association, a clique if I can say that. I yearned to feel better about myself but was not ready to go as far as some of my peers would. I was confused about the things I did and did not like about myself. When people used to say "Wow, you're so unique!", it reinforced my already preconceived sense of being patronised and my need to ask "Unique? In what regard?" It didn't feel like a compliment to me, it only highlighted the fact that I was "odd", not "normal".

If only I had known, back then, that to make and cause the most change in the world, you only need to be you. No one has ever caused change by trying to fit in.

There is beauty in being different
I did try to be different at some stage of my teenage years due to my many insecurities but I came back to the conclusion that being different like I was, wasn't bad after all. I read somewhere that "An apple could never be an orange on the inside. That doesn't mean anything is wrong with the apple." I completely agree with that statement. I found people along my journey who genuinely appreciated who I was and as I grew older I had a

better relationship with those around me as I made peace with who I am.

Do I still think I'm adopted? Do I still feel like I don't belong? Is my dad the next Indiana Jones? The answer to all those questions is a resounding "No". I've come to the conclusion that I am perfect just the way I am, I have embraced the fact that I am different and I believe I am a perfect fit for my family.

I would like you to take a moment to picture the pieces of a jigsaw (just envision it). Those pieces are not all of the same shape and size but they all fit together to make a beautiful picture and that's how we are as a family but also as children of God. We cannot all be the same, that would be pretty boring, right!? We all have a role and purpose to play within our family, community, and life in general.

I think this is an opportune time for a truth bomb you deserve to hear, in case you have been struggling with it, you didn't choose the family you were born or raised in. It was not your choice, therefore, I plead with you to know that irrespective of your experiences, they are a story and a means to greater and stronger times ahead. Only if you recognise that. Once you know and understand your purpose, you understand the reason for your peculiar characteristics and your specific interests. Who you are is not a mistake, nothing about you is a mistake.

You, as an individual, are unique in every possible way! Embrace your difference! Thinking that you should be like anyone else is a big mistake. So what if you do not fit in a box - boxes are usually created by Man and society to stifle you. The most successful people didn't make it by trying to fit in a box. Celebrate yourself even if no one else does. You have to live your life fulfilling your own destiny and not trying to conform. We were all made unique for a purpose only we can fulfil on this earth.

Chapter 3
Against all odds

Despite the many challenges of my childhood, I surely can say I did pretty well – survived and achieved despite the odds stacked against me – in my teenage years until the fateful day my mum passed away which was a tipping point for me.

Suicidal thoughts

I first had suicidal thoughts when I was 12 years old. I was in a bad place emotionally as my emotions constantly fluctuated from one end of the spectrum to the other. I was sad, really sad.

One day, in foster care, I started hearing voices out of the blue, daring me to end my life. For a while, I managed to block the voices but when my mum passed away, in a moment of weakness, I allowed them in. I just had to listen to what they were saying.

I was 13 years old when my mum passed away. She hadn't been well for a while as mentioned earlier nevertheless this was unexpected. She had managed to get us all out of "the system" a couple of months before she passed away. We were finally living with our mum from October 1996 until she passed away in April 1997. She was 34 years old.

I remember that day like it was yesterday. The week before she passed away, I got home from school and my sister was on the phone to the ambulance service. I quickly understood it was about our mum. I hurried to see our mum in her bedroom, she was conscious but didn't look very well. I selfishly didn't think she needed me around so after checking on her I waited in the living room until the ambulance crew arrived. They took her that day and I said goodbye expecting to see her in a couple of days. I never imagined that it would be the last time I saw her. The week after, I was in a science class, I was asked out of the class and instructed to go home.

On my way home, the thought that my mum passed away crossed my mind but I didn't want to think about it instead I started thinking about other reasons that would warrant my need to return home. I thought maybe they had found my secret diary (every little girl had one) and I was about to be questioned and beaten over what was written. I mostly used my diary to vent or write about my secret crushes, mind you there were not many crushes but many pages about this "Paul" who was 2 years my senior. Just the thought of those pages being read out back to me made me nervously sick. That was definitely worth a beating I guess.

I went home as quick as I could but to my surprise no one was at home. Because our landline phone wasn't working, I went to the nearest pharmacy and asked if I could make a phone call. I instinctively called my great uncle who lived 10 minutes away from us. He told me to head to their house so I did, it was a long walk.

As I approached their building, I could see a lot of people / family members out on the balcony. My heart started racing and I started feeling sick. My thoughts were all meddled up as I slowly made my way into the elevator and to their front door. I walked in, the first thing I saw on my left was my big sister curled up on the sofa. I went around the house to greet everyone. I passed my little sister, the one straight after me, who seemed "normal" but the atmosphere wasn't how it should be. It was heavy and tense.

Uncles and aunties were in the bedrooms crying. One of my uncles sat me down and I could tell from the look on his face I was about to hear some rather tough and difficult news which he had a hard time telling me. As soon as I sat down, without any warning, he said, "Your mum passed away this morning." My mind went blank. At that instant, my big sister let out a loud cry which got our little sister crying but I was numb. I ran outside because I needed some air.

My uncle lived on the 6th floor of a tall building. I stood by the balcony and stared at the road below. My thoughts were "Am I brave enough to jump?" "What if I jump but don't die?" "Will I die straight away?". I wanted to jump, I really wanted to. I can't remember how long I stayed there staring but it felt like a very long time. Then I started running. I ran and ran and ran like a lunatic. I wanted to "die". I felt like a coward for not having the courage to jump that day. During this period of grief, the pain was too much and I often found myself staring at objects such as knives and with a deep propensity to grab them and cut myself or on other occasions whilst walking down the road a sudden urge to cross the road to be ran over. I would walk and elaborate plans in my head that would result in the "perfect" death. I saw death opportunities everywhere I was. My mind was stuck on "death" mode for a very long time after receiving the most dreadful news.

I could see death opportunities everywhere. I had flashes in my mind seeing myself dead. At times, the voices were daring me and so loud I could not hear myself think. They were overwhelming and constantly talking. I also remember seeing shadows in the dark and being scared. Then one day, it all stopped.

Later on, we were told she was in a coma for a couple of days but before she took her last breath, she shed a tear.

Living arrangements

Before our mum's casket was flown to Congo, a ceremony was held at our family church which my siblings and I were unable to attend by choice. We had a few traumatic and emotional days from the moment we got the news. After our mum's remains were repatriated to Congo to be buried, the logistics of our lives began. The elders of the family had a meeting to discuss "the orphans". From my understanding, no one was prepared to take on 4 children, understandably, so they decided to split us into 2. Two of us went to live with my aunt - mum's little sister and my other siblings to my mum's uncle, our great uncle.

Meeting my dad for the "first" time

About one or two weeks after my mum passed away I met my dad. He must have heard of her passing and came to pay his respect. That was quite unexpected but they had history and she was the mother of his daughter. When he arrived at my aunt's house, he first had to speak to my uncles and aunts before he was welcomed and introduced to me. Although he got emotional when he saw me, I felt nothing. It may sound harsh but it is the truth, to me he was a stranger. I wished I had met him under better circumstances. There were not a lot of words to say to each other; I did not have much to say and I could not tell if he felt the same. And if he did, they were never spoken. He brought back memories of letters we had exchanged in the past. We had lost touch because my mum moved a lot. From his letters, I knew he lived in London but I wasn't curious to know him. He informed me he was married and had children meaning I had younger siblings. He went on to tell me more about his family and I found it very bizarre when he referred to his children as to "your brother" "your sister" because to me my family was my sisters who I grew up with and those who have seen me grow up.

When he got back to London, we continued writing to each other. He would send money and gifts (he never missed a birthday). We had very awkward phone calls but then got more comfortable as we found more things to talk about. He would send me pictures of his family which I thought he was pushing on me a bit too much, especially when he suggested that I call my step mum "mum". "No, thank you!", I thought, I already have a mum.

On occasions when we spoke, he would pass the phone to her and my siblings but as hard as we tried we had nothing to say to each other. Firstly, they spoke English so our conversations were usually 3 liners. Secondly, we were complete strangers. I think at that time, I just wanted to get to know him, no one else.

He was committed to getting to know me and made numerous attempts to get to know me to meet his family (I know I sound really detached but that was then) thus, paid for my first trip to London a year later. From then on, he consistently asked me to come and live with him. He really wanted a relationship with me and I wasn't sure how I really felt about it. Bottom line, I wasn't prepared to leave my sisters and family for the unknown.

In summer 1998, I finally made that trip to London, I met my "other" family and they made my stay very pleasant and welcoming. My dad spoiled me, I had never been spoiled before so it must admit it was nice. I suddenly felt like a priority in someone's life and he made sure I knew that. Their family dynamic was something I always wanted, a mum and a dad. I stayed with them for a couple of weeks then. During that time, I managed to form a great bond with my siblings, mostly with the girls.

Dark moments

Going back to Toulouse, I was still living with my aunt and it was not easy at all. She wouldn't let me grieve my mum's passing. She used to get upset with me if she saw me crying so I was told not to cry because that would upset my little sister too. How can you tell a child, your niece, to not mourn her mother? I had to hide to cry and kept it that way for a while. As long as I looked happy on the outside, we were good I guess. I had no one to turn or run to. I would assume my aunt's attempt at helping me deal with the grief was buying me everything I asked for when we first moved in, yet she was still insensitive to my pain and never entertained a discussion about my mother. Yes, she had lost a sister but she had years with her which we didn't. I played a bit on the fact that I would get the things that I wanted but deep down I started thinking "What's the point of life anyway?" From then my thoughts became very dark again and I found myself contemplating death again. "Yes, that's clearly the easy way out," I thought to myself.

The first time I played to the tune of these dark thoughts, I was at my lowest sitting in a park. I found a broken glass on the ground, picked it up and started looking at my wrist. The voices inside my head once again became louder than my own, daring me to slash my wrists. I took the broken glass and started attempting to scratch my wrist until I saw blood coming out. I dug the glass a bit deeper each time. I'm not sure what I was thinking as I was doing it but the pain made me stop. I could hear the voices mocking me. I felt so stupid and hid what I had done. No one knew. It was my little secret. I covered the injury until it healed and that was it.

On another dark day, in the late afternoon, as I was going through the motions, I dared myself, "Why not now?". Thoughts came rushing through my head as I went through our pharmacy cupboards and took a box of over the counter painkillers. I had to make it quick and for a successful result, I thought I'd drink those pills with some cheap perfume I had. I closed my bedroom door and sat on the edge of my bed staring at the empty white wall in front of me until I was completely lost in my thoughts.

I felt really sorry for myself and as tears streamed down my cheeks I started shoving pills down my throat, not one, not two but the whole lot (I think there were about 8), and drank some of the perfume. The taste was awful!

My little cousin walked in on me and stood in shock. He started crying and pleading with me to stop as I was tilting the bottle of perfume in my mouth. Horrified by what was happening, he quickly took the rest of the painkillers which were by my side and snatched the perfume bottle from my hand. I tearfully looked at him and held my head as I started feeling dizzy. In panic, he ran out to call his mum.

My aunt calmly came in, looked at me and said "If you want to die, not in my house" then she walked out. I don't even think I reacted to her words. Yes, maybe I was seeking attention but I was a broken child who had recently lost her mum. I started crying again and shouted at my cousin to leave me alone.

My head started spinning faster so I laid down on my bed. It was like a force was weighing my body down. I suddenly couldn't move. I stayed in the bedroom the whole afternoon and didn't come out for dinner in the evening. I just laid there with my eyes closed and eventually fell asleep. Because of the way I was feeling, I thought that maybe, just maybe I'll die in my sleep that night. To me, it was pretty clear that no one would miss me anyway.

The next morning, I was so disappointed when I woke up though my body felt like I had been run over by a truck. I went through what had happened the day before, the feelings I had and it didn't make sense to me that I would still be alive after drinking painkillers with perfume. At that point, I thought that God was keeping me alive to punish me. "That's not fair!" I foolishly said as I held back my tears. For once, I had the courage to carefully execute my most perfect plan and the result was completely contrary to what I had expected. I felt cheated. I was downhearted that even death didn't want me. It looked so easy in the movies. I felt like a failure.

Going through anorexia
From then on, I thought I'll starve myself to death. For me, that was the ultimate genius plan so from one day to the other I completely stopped eating.

Initially, when I stopped eating, no one at home noticed. I guess to them I was being a moody or hormonal teenager. After a couple of months, it became apparent that I was losing weight which caused my aunt to commence a tirade of constant criticisms and comments. When it finally became clear to her that I hadn't been eating, she took me to the doctor as I had lost a considerable amount of weight. I wasn't overweight but I had become thinner and my collar bone started to show a bit more.

From his consultation, the doctor diagnosed me with anorexia[3]. I didn't think there was a name for this. At nearly 16, I weighed about 40kg. The doctor and my aunt sat there discussing an action plan seemingly but intentionally oblivious to my presence in the room. As we were leaving, I received a stern warning from the doctor implying that a further loss of weight (5Kg or more) could lead to being hospitalised. He, therefore, encouraged me to start eating healthily and also recommended that my aunt obtain counselling for me. Let me tell you that I did not receive counselling as it had been highly suggested and in hindsight felt that my aunt was ashamed as it would give the impression to our family, her friends and colleagues that she was unable to take care of me or I was being a nuisance to gain attention.

The days that followed our visit to the doctor, I still wasn't compliant to my aunt's demands for me to eat. There was no way my plan was going to fail. Often anorexia is referred to as an obsessive desire to lose weight by refusing to eat but in my case, I wasn't doing this to lose weight, I was determined to die.

During this time, I noticed my bones had become very fragile and fractured my ankle and wrist a few times.

Because I would not cooperate with my aunt and the doctor, my aunt proceeded to involve the school. Behind my back, she booked an appointment with the headteacher and my form tutor, to share the ordeal. I was very annoyed with her and felt like she was playing the victim. Why

[3] An eating disorder characterized by markedly reduced appetite or total aversion to food. Anorexia is a serious psychological disorder. It is a condition that goes well beyond out-of-control dieting. Anorexia can be life-threatening.

was she so bothered since she wasn't even nice to me in the first place? Anyway, together, like a rescue team planning a rescue mission, they elaborated a plan which they thought should get me back on track and presented it to me. I was very upset. I didn't think it was my aunt's place to tell but I also felt like she made it all about her. From then on, all my teachers were aware of my condition and a few of my close friends had to be involved. Suddenly, it felt like everyone knew. I hated that feeling. I became angrier with my aunt. Her caring attitude was so fake and unnecessary. "She's ruined it all!", I thought to myself.

For their plan, a couple of my close friends were designated to sit with me at lunchtime in the cafeteria to ensure that I ate. I had priority to enter the cafeteria before anyone, so we jumped the queue. I was not allowed back in class until I had eaten something. I thought that since my friends were involved, I'd be able to get away with not eating but little did I know, my friends were very committed. For example, I would try to bribe my friends into telling the teachers that I had eaten but they did not support this. Lunchtime became painful for me and a moment I dreaded when getting into school. There were times I would stare at the food on my plate the entire lunch hour and still eat nothing. Our afternoon class would have started and we were still in the cafeteria. On one occasion, one of my friends burst into tears while pleading with me to eat a piece of bread. I didn't want to break down in tears so I kept staring at the food on my plate. "What if you die?" she shouted at me. I shrugged and replied "I don't care." I was stubborn.

No one understood why I would do that to myself as I looked so happy, I had a lot of friends and my school results were excellent. I excelled academically causing the teachers to wonder what the real issue was. It was a dilemma – a puzzle they could not solve.

We became regulars at our doctor's surgery. Both the doctors and the school suggested that I see a psychotherapist but my aunt was still against the idea, so I was never seen in the clinic, apart from the doctor checking my weight every 2 weeks.

There is a notion that people of African origin are averse to counselling or therapy of every type mostly due to the stigma associated with it. And this was no isolated case.

Similar to life at school, at home, my cousin was my warden at meal times. I remember sitting at the table until midnight with my plate untouched. My aunt had enough of me so I was reluctantly sent to bed. It was obviously very late and I had school the next day; for me that was a victory. Sad, isn't it!

My aunt's husband seemed disinterested or dare I say nonchalant about me or my upbringing. In hindsight, I am of the strong opinion he was uninvolved in the decision to relocate my sister and I to theirs and our upbringing in their care. He was not involved in anything concerning me.

Most of my family were not aware of what I was going through and I think my aunt preferred it that way - she may not have wanted anyone to know she was incapable of bringing up her sister's children. When I visited family, they would constantly comment on my weight and how skinny I looked. I couldn't confide in my big sister regarding my struggles because I thought it was unfair on her as she seemed to be going through her own stuff and she seemed happy. I didn't want to be a bother so I decided that I was alone on this journey.

After 6 months, I had enough of waiting to die by starvation and I could clearly see that God didn't want me otherwise He would have sped up the process. Well, that's what I thought. I would go to bed every night feeling weaker and thinking "This is it world, see you never!". But after a while, I got used to the headaches and the emptiness I felt in my stomach. My whole body had become used to not being fed and I am not sure I was drinking that much water or any other liquids at the time.

Every time I saw our family doctor he would look alarmed and would threaten to have me hospitalised. He knew that at a point, for my safety, he would have no option but to have me sectioned/admitted into hospital.

If I am honest, I didn't want to be hospitalised because I didn't actually think that I had a problem, plus it would have been a hospital specialised with mental health issues. "I'm not crazy!" I thought to myself. So one day, I am not sure what triggered this but I ate a small morsel of food. I think seeing and hearing my friends, my teachers and those who cared about me being so crushed made me realise how selfish I was. My sisters needed me, we needed each other. How would they feel losing me? Was I really ready to die?

When I started eating again, though very small portions, I could feel every bit of food dropping in my empty stomach. And every time I ate, no matter how small the portion was, I would be in excruciating pain. I don't think I have ever experienced such stomach pain before. I felt sick. It came to a point when I would eat and tear up because of the pain. The pain, for a couple of weeks, was unbearable. I explained this to the doctor who explained that my stomach had shrunk, that was probably the best way for me to understand. He then prescribed some medicine to alleviate the pain. Eating had become such a chore! The previous episode of me taking medication with perfume had possibly aggravated the situation but I had not mentioned this to the doctor on any of our visits.

Reflecting through pain

I had suffered in silence for over a year, though I knew what I was doing wasn't right, all I wanted was for the deep searing pain to end. Terrible anguish struck my heart at the thought of forgetting what my mum looked like. At times, I could not remember her face but only remember her perfume and the red lipstick she so beautifully wore. It tore at me physically, mentally and emotionally. I couldn't talk about my mum, I couldn't cry. The pain had its hands around my heart, choking me. My cry for help was silenced to the world. I felt I was on my own and that's where my thoughts brewed and took over my mind. I felt alone and lonely most of the time. In a place of loneliness, thoughts are not usually positive and once I gave in to them, everything spiralled out of control. I was out of control even though I felt like I was in control. Nothing made sense. The devil had me locked in the prison of my morbid thoughts. Was death really my only option?

From the moment our mum passed away, we should have received some sort of counselling but I have come to understand from experience of living in an African home, going to see a counsellor is not always what parents would suggest or agree to. Very often mental health is unspoken of in African families and as a result people suffer in silence. Sadly, some may find death the easier option just like I thought it could be for me. But my advice is to not look at what is culturally acceptable in this case and seek help, hang on to life and find help. Talk, find people who would listen to you. When it comes to mental health it is somehow easier to talk to strangers (i.e. counsellor or psychotherapist) which some African parents can't seem to be able to deal with "how can you expose your/our life to a complete stranger!". At times, the fact that you are seeking help elsewhere makes them feel as if they have failed or worse as if they are incompetent. Chances are, they will make it about them and not you. Nevertheless, don't let that stop you from seeking the help you need. You can also try to understand what triggers your negative thought patterns and how to overcome them. Don't give up, don't give in.

Looking back at all I did, I feel really bad because I was only thinking about myself. I just wanted to die and that was it! It took me a few years to go back to a healthy weight and because of the anorexia, I had lost my appetite and at times I would not eat for 3/4 days before realising I hadn't eaten. I had to force and remind myself to have 3 meals a day.

After all this, I did have many other battles in my mind, but I knew to not entertain them anymore. The door to unhelpful thinking had been wide open for such a long time, I had to find enough mental strength to close it for good. I could have died so many times and although I thought God was conspiring against me, I have come to understand that He was protecting me from myself. Today I stand as proof that when God has a plan and a purpose for your life, He would not let any harm come to you (Psalm 121:7 - The LORD will keep you from all harm - he will watch over your life.)

I thank God for the friends I had back then who didn't give up on me even when I threatened to end our friendship (childish), they stuck by me. With unwavering hope and resilience, they could muster at our age, they stood by me to see me through a rather tough time. God bless them. We all need friends like this - who hold you accountable and love you enough to tell you the hard truths and walk with you to recovery and growth. Thinking that you are alone is a state of mind because we are never really alone. As Christians, we understand that God is always with us but if not that, understand that God has assigned friendships / relationships that would benefit you in time of need.

For all the reasons above and after experiencing such tragedies and traumas at an earlier stage in life, I realised I had to mature faster than some of my peers. I seemed to always be a step ahead.

Early independence

As previously stated, I was living with my aunt, my mum's sister, after my mum passed away. Living there was certainly not easy and every day I felt like I was sinking into a black hole with no sign of an exit. This was all happening on the inside and apart from the suicide attempts and the anorexia no one knew the depths of my thoughts.

In summer 2000, I was 17, my aunt sent me to Paris on holiday to visit my uncle, my mum's cousin. I was happy because it meant that I would be going with my big sister and cousin. It was a good summer for us as we got to spend time together. We also got to meet up with some famous Congolese singers my cousin had met the previous summer during her holiday in Congo as she had kept in touch with them. If you are Congolese, you would recognise some of those artists' names. That summer, we were out and about every day and we were very excited to be allowed to attend amazing events including a couple of concerts on our own but also with our uncle who was highly supportive of our daily trips. It was an opportunity for us to build rapport and friendships.

At the end of the summer, there was a concert we really wanted to go to and we knew that one of our uncles would be able to get us in for free. We discussed it with him and he promised to take us but the problem was that my return ticket to Toulouse was the day before. The uncle we were staying with called my aunt to tell her that he was going to change my ticket and that I will be back in a couple of days after the original date. She seemed ok with it but when he passed the phone to me she said with a serious voice that when I was back in Toulouse I was not welcome in her house.

At first I thought she was joking and so did my uncle when I told him but when I got back to Toulouse the word had already gone round. She was very serious. Because I was starting high school a couple of days after our arrival, I went to stay with my mum's uncle, my great uncle, where my 2 other sisters lived. The problem was, their 4 bedroom flat was overcrowded – my uncle and his wife, their 5 children, my 2 sisters and 2 other uncles lived there. An overcrowded flat was an understatement as there was always someone visiting for a couple of days or weeks. I could not live there for more than a few weeks. My great uncle did pay for my school stationery as I had nothing to start school with. The only clothes I had were those I had worn throughout the summer. I was very sad, rejected and could not understand the reason behind my aunt's decision. She never called to check up on me. Everyone carried on with their life as if it was normal. After a week or so, I was sent to live with my maternal uncle.

I stayed at my uncle's for a week then one day out of the blue he took me back to my aunt despite the fact that he knew she didn't want me there. I was so cross with him because they had tried to reason with her and she stood her ground, she didn't want me back! It didn't make sense.

They were now forcing me on her and she made sure I knew that I was no longer wanted in her house. One day, as I had had enough of her treatments, I took it upon myself to contact social services because the atmosphere at home was unbearable. We ended up going to court and I was placed in a temporary flat awaiting a place in a care home as I was a minor. I remember my aunt fuming and threatening me as I was packing my bags to go. She had absolutely no reason to do what she did or react the way she did. I wasn't welcome to stay so I left.

I started living on my own from the age of 17. This was very strange for me. I had my own little flat in the town centre right next to my high school. Although I was happier, I could not stop thinking about my little sister whom I had left behind. To be spiteful, my aunt didn't allow me to see her and that broke my heart. I had lost all contact with her but when it was time to find work experience in spring 2001, I found a place that was right next to my little sister's school. I would visit her on my lunch break. The school staff were very kind to allow me to see her but I had to warn them and her not to inform my aunt. The ladies were very accommodating and understanding of the situation. We were very happy to see each other. Imagine not seeing someone you used to live with for such a long time! My work experience was only 2 weeks and we made the most of it.

I mentioned previously that my aunt was very good at playing the victim so for a while most of my family were upset with me. I avoided gatherings and kept to myself.

The flat I lived in was paid for. Rather than receiving money for food, I was given restaurant vouchers which had a maximum amount to spend in specific restaurants. My favourite one at the time was McDonalds. I think at that time, I had

McDonalds for lunch and dinner. You couldn't spend those vouchers on anything else which was really sad for me. They also bought me a plane ticket to go visit my dad during the Christmas holiday.

My caseworker was amazing. When I got back from London in January 2001, I was moved into a care home which for me meant back to sharing a room and back to the routine but it was good somehow. I wasn't used to living on my own and it had become very boring as all my friends had family to go back to. I needed people around. They explained that I would be moved to another care home when I turn 18, which was in a couple of months, shortly after I would be given a flat to become more independent. I was one of the oldest in that first care home and at first I just stayed on my own. I was a full time student working a part time weekend job as a healthcare assistant in a hospital. It meant I had no time to socialise and at first I had no desire to. I thought to myself there was no need to get to know anyone as I was not going to stay there for very long. I was allocated a room to share with another girl who later on became my best friend.

Academically, I was still doing good, what I had been through had no affected my learning. The fact that I was working meant that I was able to save some money and spend some on the things I liked. Managing my own money made me a bit more independent.

I moved into my own flat a couple of months after my 18th birthday. I made sure to celebrate my 18th birthday the best way I could, by hiring a hall and partied all night with friends, my sister and cousins. By that time, things had settled with my family though things remained the same with my aunt, she is as stubborn as I am.

At 19, I got my baccalaureate and celebrated another school achievement. This was great! I had finally finished studying and waiting here back from the universities I had applied to. I was in a much better place mentally.

That summer, I resigned from my part time weekend job at the hospital to enjoy the summer holidays. During summer when university places were announced, I had still not received an offer to any of the ones I had applied to which was very disappointing. I wrote a few appeal letters but nothing became available by September. By mid September, I started working full time as a healthcare assistant in a nursing home. It wasn't ideal but it was fun and it paid well. My big sister's friend, who is now like a sister to me, put in a good word for me to start working with her. I will discuss the details of this friendship in the next chapter.

At my age working full time in a nursing home wasn't very popular and I did think that there was more to me than what I was doing so one evening I made the decision that I would be better off to go live with my dad. I announced it to my caseworker and we went back and forth over the pros and cons though my mind was set. When I told my dad, he was very happy.

Mid November 2002, I took a leap of faith and gave my landlord notice and started packing. It was a big move because I had to ship all my stuff to London. There would be nothing to go back to except visiting my siblings and family.

On the day, before heading to the airport, I had few stops to make but one was very important to me. I went to my aunt's to bid my little sister farewell. I had not been there in such a long time and I was unsure what to expect. They were surprised to see me, but I had to do it. On our way back to the car, I spoke briefly with my aunt and also apologised to her. Although I knew she had hurt me, I felt the need to apologise to her for how I had hurt her too. I wasn't expecting anything from her anymore, time had passed and I had made my peace with the situation. I believed strength and growth are evident in recognising that you may never receive an apology from someone however, you do what is needed to bring freedom and I wanted to be free.

My aunt and I did have a conversation after many years about what had happened as I still needed to understand the reason why she had done what she did. She explained that I had undermined her authority by staying in Paris that summer when she had planned for us to prepare for everything I needed to start high school. Though this, to me, wasn't a good reason, I had made my peace with what had happened and we never spoke about this again.

Those friends who become family
My big sister had a good friend, whom she went boarding school with, who quickly became part of our family as she would spend weeks on end at our great uncle's house where my big sister lived. Her family lived near Bordeaux which is north of Toulouse and when she wasn't there she was with us.

As I mentioned earlier, she quickly became part of the family and when she decided to settle in Toulouse, we ended up living together in my little studio flat and that is how we became close. I considered her my friend too.

The summer of 2002 was a good summer for us as it was filled with spontaneous travelling opportunities/decisions. We would just up and go without a care in the world. I mentioned earlier that we worked together and we had so much fun working and living together. Though we enjoyed our work, it became somehow tiring so by October, we wanted to move on. She decided to become an au pair and was approached by a family in London. She was very excited and getting herself ready for her big move. A couple of weeks passed and I started contemplating the idea of moving to London myself. I thought that would be a good opportunity to bond with my dad and siblings. By the end of November, we were both ready for this new adventure though we knew we wouldn't be together but it was still a comfort for us to have someone we knew in town.

Leaving for the unknown
The day of our departure, we travelled around Toulouse to say our final goodbyes to friends and family. We were excited and anxious at the same time. This was majorly big for us. We both never really lived that far from our families.

On the plane, we took selfies and probably were the only ones bouncing around in excitement. Because she knew she would have her weekends free, we started planning what we would be doing and how often we'll get to see each other. I hoped that my family in London would welcome her the same way my family in Toulouse had welcomed her because as far as I was concerned she is family.

When we landed, it was time to say our goodbyes to each other as she was picked up by her au pair family and I was picked up by dad. I did introduce her to my dad and she introduced me to her au pair family. We referred to each other as "cousins" which we have been doing ever since. After a brief chat between all of us, we went our separate ways. I think the first few weeks we found it hard to settle into this new life. Keeping in constant contact helped us a lot. Then we settled and started college to improve our English. She spent some weekends at ours and when I settled in a church, we started attending the same church. We were there for each other.

Getting to know my other family

Let me tell you that living with people and visiting them are 2 different things. I had been around my siblings every time I visited London and we had good times yet when I came to live with them it was different from what I had experienced and expected. My little brothers were not very kind to me, especially the eldest who made sure I knew I was not part of their family. He even managed to make me cry on a couple of occasions. I even remember one Christmas he tried to fight with me. I felt alone and most of the time missing the family I had left behind. I missed my sisters and my friends. I found it hard to adjust knowing I was far away from familiar faces.

My dad did everything he could to make me feel at home and welcome but he was busy at work so his younger brother, my uncle, who also lived in London, would take me out every chance he got. It was a joy to have my uncle around most days. He is not much older than me so I don't call him uncle but "ya" which is a prefix we use in Congo to call our older siblings. To my surprise, his girlfriend started making defamatory comments about my uncle and I being in a relationship. What a twisted mind! I thought she was wicked for even thinking that. He is the big brother I always wanted and we bonded straight away. I got on with him more than I did with my dad at the time.

My relationship with my dad would be what most people would term as normal. However, from past hurts and not having lived with him, as far as I could remember, I found his care and affection overbearing hence I did not respond well to the fatherly protectiveness, kindness and love.

After a few months, even though I got used to having this new family around, I still missed and desired to be with the family I grew up around. I would often cry in secret or cry on the phone to my big sister. I would even call my aunt, yes my aunt!, to complain and cry. "Come back to Toulouse" she told me but I thought it would not make any sense as I had nowhere to go if I did go back.

Despite my dad's best efforts, he could see that I was unhappy. Once again, I felt like I did not belong. I was reminded that I was the daughter he had with someone else, especially when my stepmum would introduce me to their friends as "his daughter" and then proceed to introduce her own children. I am not sure why I felt that way because she wasn't lying but it reinforced my sense of not belonging. I felt like she didn't need to make that point to others.

I must admit that it was hard for me to bond with my dad. I was 19 and I didn't know how to relate to him or be around him. Looking back, I can clearly see that I wasn't making any real effort to get to know him as I kept my focus on the side of the family I knew and grew up with. Another reason why I didn't make any effort to bond with him was because he was very critical of my mum. Though the life she lived was far from perfect and she did make some wrong choices at times, I have no doubt that she loved us. It seemed like my dad had nothing nice to say about my mum and he sounded really bitter over their past. She wasn't here to defend herself or give her version of events, so it wasn't fair and I didn't want him to constantly speak so negatively about her. "Can you not talk about her like that! She never said anything bad about you." I once blurred out. I didn't want him to spoil my memories of her.

My dad was very patient with me and bought me return tickets to Toulouse most school holidays the first year I arrived in London so that I could visit my maternal family and friends. He knew that would make me happy so he didn't hesitate. I needed those time away as I seemed to be having a mini depression.

I didn't want to feel the way I felt but I couldn't help it. I knew I had to do something about it, so I kept repeating to myself "at least I have a dad." I know it sounds foolish but having my dad meant that I wasn't an orphan, so I thought. My maternal sisters and I all have our dads but none of them were in touch with theirs at the time so I didn't want to be ungrateful. Plus, I'm not a quitter so I pulled myself together and opened up a little bit more every day for my new family to know me.

My early years as a Christian
I grew up in a Christian family but I can't say that I knew what being a Christian was back then or even who God really was. Growing up, I have vague memories of doing catechism in the Catholic Church, not sure who took us there but those were my references to God.

Most of my family are Christians, though some of their actions from what you read above may not reflect this, but they are, remember no one is perfect. One of my mum's uncles is a pastor so in Toulouse we were used to attending church every Sunday. We even had to sing in the church choir but this was more of a chore than a love for Christ. We had to be at church as a family and that was it.

In my older/latter teenage years, my sister, cousins and I would go clubbing on Saturday evening and still turn up to the Sunday morning service. It was more of a duty – we knew we would get in trouble if we didn't attend so even with our sleepy eyes we were there. Being there was what mattered but we were not paying much attention. I cannot recall if any messages preached ever got to me or even if the gospel of Christ was presented to me with the opportunity to give my life to Christ. In all honesty, I don't think I would have been ready to take that leap of faith at that time. I was a logical person and I sort of questioned everything, the type to only believe in what I could see.

Our mum took us religiously to church whenever we spent our weekends with her and more regularly once we got to live with her. Her faith kept growing stronger as the sickness weakened her. She clearly loved God and got baptised the year she died. She gave a heartfelt testimony that day and I still have a picture of her from that day. She looked so beautiful in her cream dress. It's a sincere comfort to me knowing that she gave her life and that one day we'll see each other again.

Coming to London, I was relieved that I was out of that chore of attending church, singing in the choir, etc. I knew my dad was not going to force me to do anything so I stayed out of church.

I started college in January 2003 where I met a lady who seemed really nice and we happened to be in the same class. The first thing she said to me was "Can I invite you to my church on Sunday?" Out of respect and probably what you would call religion, I couldn't say no but I was not impressed. That Sunday, I met her at Southgate tube station and we walked to the church. It was a lovely little church and it was my first time attending a church service in London. I had to stay focused on every word the pastor spoke in his sermon as my English was not yet as fluent as it is now. I understood more than I could speak but the kind of English we learned at school was definitely not the same that people spoke out there. To my surprise, I really enjoyed the service more than I thought I would; I somehow felt connected and kept going back every Sunday. I even took my little sisters there one day. The pastor and his wife were lovely and welcoming.

In April 2003, I moved to a hostel in Bayswater at the advice of my uncle's girlfriend at the time who thought it would be a good idea for me to have my own place. I wasn't against the idea as I was used to living on my own and the sleeping arrangements at my dad were not great. I also thought maybe having some space from each other may help us all to have a better relationship.

Despite the distance, I kept going to the same church, they had become like family to me. I was still attending college too, even though this meant a 1h30 journey by bus, I was happy to travel across London. After a while, I decided to tell the pastor's wife about my move to Central London as I could not keep up with the Sunday services. My last Sunday there, she made sure to pray for me, and there and then I spoke in tongues[4] for the first time.

The following week I was contacted by a lady from Kensington Temple London City Church (KTLCC). My pastor had contacted their church to inform them of my move and he wanted me to start attending a local church rather than travelling across London every Sunday. The lady explained what/who Kensington Temple is and suggested that on Sunday we meet and together attend the English speaking service and then the French speaking service. I was excited to know that I had a language option. That Sunday, I was at Kensington Temple a.k.a KT but I had never been in a big church. It was overwhelming for me and I

---

[4] Speaking in tongues is a spiritual gift that can be manifested as either a human language or a heavenly supernatural language.

felt like a small fish in the ocean. It was too big! When I visited the French speaking church, Pierres Vivantes, it was smaller and there were fewer people so I automatically felt more comfortable and decided to start attending there. From then on, I would only attend KT when we had corporate meetings of all satellite churches.

I loved the church services and the community. In a short period of time I drew closer to God like I had never been before and was baptised at KT in September 2003 after attending an Encounter (a weekend spiritual retreat) for the first time. This was a big decision for me and I intended to stay on the right path this time as I had no one forcing me to do anything, this was my own decision.

I attended Pierres Vivantes regularly and became a children's ministry leader which I enjoyed. I thought I had found my way with God and this made me very happy. I wasn't just sitting around in church as I used to; I was part of the church, part of the family / community. When I moved to Luton for work purposes I would still take the train down every Sunday to attend service and occasionally on Thursday for our weekly cell meetings.

I never really had a personal experience of God as such but I knew that God exists, though I had moments of doubts, deep down I knew. I was determined to take my walk with Him seriously this time. At the encounter a lot of deliverance happened and I wanted to experience more of the freedom I had found.

Hearing God for the first time
Early 2004, I was involved in a serious car accident which could have been fatal for me. It happened around Borehamwood and it was a head to head collision. My colleague and I were driving back to Luton after a long day of work in

Borehamwood. When I got in the car, I was so annoyed and exhausted by the day we had and sat in the front passenger seat without putting my seatbelt on.

As soon as she started driving, I fell into an unusual deep sleep. I say unusual because I am not a deep sleeper. Whilst in deep sleep, I heard a gentle voice telling me to put my seatbelt on. Suddenly, it was as if there was a battle in my mind as I recall not wanting to wake up. Minutes later, I heard the same voice again but a bit more insisting asking me to put my seatbelt on and the same battle was happening in my mind as I felt like if I woke up my sleep would be disrupted. It was the kind of sleep you really enjoy especially after a long and hard day's work. The third time I heard the voice, it was louder and very firm so I jumped up and put my seatbelt on and went back to that deep sleep straight away. Not even 1 minute after putting my seatbelt on, we were involved in a head to head accident. Let me tell you that if I hadn't put my seatbelt on, I would have gone through our car windscreen and landed on or in the other car but God is good. My right wrist was injured by the impact of the accident so I had to be taken to the hospital. My friend kept retelling how the way I quickly got up and put on my seatbelt looked "crazy" but we were both thankful that nothing too serious happened. That's when I understood that I had just heard God's voice. The side roads in Borehamwood do meander and are also quite steep; the accident happened whilst my friend was manoeuvring one of these turns.

After that accident, I was signed off work and moved back to London to work as an au pair for a family I knew and from there moved into a hostel in West London.

Chapter 4
With every heartbreak

Recently, I heard the saying "Sometimes we make broken choices out of a broken place" It made me realise I never really took time to heal from my childhood, my mother's death and from what I had been through with my aunt and in moment of forging a new life and beginning, all those negative feelings resurfaced.

Troubled memories

I would like to take you back to a time in my childhood which affected me in a way I never imagined. From what you have read, nothing has ever been very straightforward for me but there were moments that changed quite a lot in me and I will go ahead and share a few of these.

One day in foster care, something quite upsetting happened to me which made me question my sexuality for a long time. I was young and naive and never actually stopped to think that evil was out there but at the age of 10, I was sexually abused while in foster care.

This girl was 16. She was in fact the eldest in the whole care home. I knew her of course because as girls we shared a dormitory but I didn't associate with her much.

One evening when all the girls had left to go downstairs for dinner and I was the last one to shower that evening. As I was coming out of the shower and walking to my bedroom, I realised I was left alone, so I thought. The girls' dormitory was on the top floor of the 4-storey house.

As I was getting dressed, she let herself in my bedroom. I thought she had come to call me for dinner but I started feeling uncomfortable as she stood there and without saying a word cornered me. She pushed me onto the bottom bed of the bunk bed I shared with my sister and pinned me down. She proceeded with the act as I was frozen in shock while she abused me. When she left, it took me a while to get dressed again then I ran downstairs to join the others at the dining table. She was already there smiling and chatting away as if nothing had happened. I couldn't look at her, I felt so dirty.

The same scenario happened on a couple of occasions after that. It felt like she was preying on me and knew the exact moments when I was alone. I felt targeted. I grew scared of being alone in the showers, in my bedroom and anywhere she could possibly find me alone but I kept silent because I was ashamed by the thought of anyone knowing. She never threatened me to keep quiet but the thought of her doing worse was enough to keep me silent and in constant fear.

On one occasion, she got herself on the bed and forced my head between her legs. The more I pulled my head back to get away, the more she pushed it in. I was disgusted. She had no underwear on and I knew what she wanted me to do but I wasn't prepared to do it. It was a wrestle which she won, though I didn't perform any act on her, my head was stuck between her legs for what seemed like hours to me as she firmly gave instructions on what she wanted me to do. I had no such desires towards her or any girls. As she was not getting her own way, she let go of me and I ran out. She defiled me in every way I could think about.

As long as she was around, I felt unsafe. I did everything I could to never find myself alone with her again then she eventually stopped. She made me sick, everything about her made me sick and made my skin crawl. I felt dirty, I was disgusted and ashamed not only by her but also with myself. I was an innocent child and she violated me. Out of fear and shame, I kept what happened to myself and never spoke about it until now. I managed to bury this memory right at the back of my mind until now because I believe it is all part of my healing process to speak it out.

For a long time after that experience I questioned my sexually "Did what she do to me made me a lesbian?", "Do I like girls?", "Did I encourage what happened?" etc. so many questions rushed through my head as a teenager especially since boys showed no romantic interest in me and I had no romantic interest in them either apart from the odd crushes which never developed into anything more. I was confused. I was ashamed about what had happened for a long time and never dealt with the negative feelings I had about myself.

My coping mechanism was to pretend it never happened until I finally managed to put it all at the back of my mind. The flashbacks of those horrible moments stopped and I moved on with my life even though it had added to my insecurities and how I viewed sexuality and my body.

A dangerous game to play
In my mid-teens, I suddenly became aware of boys' interest in me which was for me a big change from constantly being in the friendzone, and in response to that attention I became flirtatious which I thought was innocent and cute at the time.

Because of what had previously happened to me, I felt like I had a point to prove to myself and flirting became something fun to me as it gave me an illusion of confidence and control. I knew that I didn't want anything more however I came to realise what a dangerous game flirting is as I got myself in some sticky situations, two of which I recall well.

On one occasion, a boy who liked me locked me in his flat. I knew he liked me for a while and we had been chatting here and there. The attention he showed me made me feel special as I had never been talked to that way before. He knew what to say and how to say it. Even though I didn't want to be his girlfriend, I still entertained the idea by flirting back.

We were both at the party house party one afternoon when he asked me to go quickly with him to his flat because he needed to pick something up. I saw nothing wrong with that so I went along as it was in the same block of flats as the party. No one was home and as soon as we got into the flat, he locked the door behind us and stood in front of it. "You'll have to kiss me to get out of here" he said. He was a bit older, much taller and evidently stronger than me. Facing him, I took a couple of steps back as I understood how serious he was by the tone of his voice. I suddenly became really scared and stood there petrified. I wanted to scream but couldn't as I was paralysed with fear. I felt sick at the thought of the many possible endings of the situation. My eyes filled with tears as I started begging him to let me out. At first, he insisted that I kiss him and came closer to grab my arms, but I cringed. He could tell from my facial expression that I wasn't comfortable at all and maybe saw the scared look in my eyes. He turned his back to me and walked back to open the door. Without saying a word, I quickly ran back to the party where my cousin was. "Where were you? I was looking for you everywhere." she said as I didn't tell anyone where I was going. "Let's go home," I softly replied pulling her towards the entrance door.

On our way back to her house, I explained my ordeal. "You're crazy!" she exclaimed. Just like me, she was horrified at the thought of what could have happened and the fact that no one knew where I was. "How can you be so careless!" she added. That evening as I laid in bed listening to my cousin telling me off, I agreed that this could have ended in a completely different way and the thought of that made me sick. I felt really stupid and not very proud of myself.

On a different occasion, in my late teens, an older guy started showing interest in, we exchanged numbers and talked for a few weeks before he asked to meet. I knew of him because he was the older brother of a girl I knew. I was definitely flattered that an older guy would show me such interest but delayed meeting him as long as I could but we eventually set a date. This guy was very handsome, he worked, had a car and I knew many girls would have killed to spend that afternoon with him so I considered myself lucky. He picked me up in the town centre and drove off. As he drove, I suddenly became aware that we were heading outside the town centre. We did not agree on where we would go that afternoon so I asked "where are we going?". He looked at me and said "to a hotel so we can be comfortable." I certainly didn't have that in mind.

My heart started racing at the thought of being with a man in a hotel but I kept my cool. I tried to keep my composure as long as I could but I was ready to jump out of his car at any minute. I hadn't told anyone I was talking to him or even meeting him that afternoon which was very silly of me. He parked at a hotel near the motorway just outside town and reassured me that we would just be talking, "nothing more," he said with a smile as he could see the look on my face. I believed him, yes I was very naive but also I didn't know how I would go back to town from there so I followed him in as he got the key to the room from the front desk. When we got in the room, I sat on the edge of the bed and to my surprise he went straight to have a shower. I was confused as it was 4pm and he didn't look like he needed a shower. After a few minutes, he came out fully naked. This was the first time I ever saw a man naked. All of a sudden what was about to happen became dawned on me. I jumped off the bed, turned my back to him as I felt uncomfortable looking at his nakedness. I was panicked on the inside but gently asked him to take me home or at least to the nearest bus stop. He sounded very surprised by my request and I couldn't blame him as I may have led him to believe that there could be more. He tried to reason with me and in a panic, I confessed that I was a virgin and couldn't go through with whatever he had in mind. "What did you want exactly!?" he said annoyingly. I didn't have an answer for him so I kept quiet. He swiftly got dressed, we walked in silence to the car and he drove me back to the care home where I lived at the time. I was mortified at the idea of what could have happened. We never saw each other again after this.

Leading people on, especially in the two instances above, could have had unpleasant outcomes. Yes, I enjoyed the attention but for the wrong reasons. I was playing with fire and nearly got burned. I knew what my intentions were in flirting with them but not theirs or maybe I did but thought I was smart enough to leave them hanging, but it's never ok to send mixed signals and play with people's feelings.

From that time, I made the decision to never find myself in such predicaments ever again. As a young girl maturing to become a young woman, I needed to learn to become more intentional and responsible in my relationships with others, especially men. I have also been at both receiving ends of mixed signals and it has never felt good. Women often complain about being led on by men but let's also be honest with the fact that we too can be the senders of those mixed signals and lead men on. Either way, this is a dangerous game to play and only leads to confusion.

Simon Rego, a psychologist and director of the Cognitive Behavior Therapy Program at Montefiore Medical Center in New York, said "Flirting is the suggestion of the possibility, but not the probability, of something sexual occurring between two individuals. It's expressed in a person's tone of voice, pauses, eye contact, posture, body language and wordplay."

As a mature Christian, I have come to understand that flirting is never as harmless as we think. There are some dangers to being a flirt:
• Flirting hurts your reputation.[5]
• Flirting hurts the person you flirt with.[6]
• Flirting hurts your prospects for genuine romance.[7]

Nowadays, I often stop to think "how is what I am doing affecting the other person?" which is overlooked when it comes to flirting as we no longer love our neighbour as ourselves and become selfish in our desire for attention.

My first proper boyfriend
I have never really been in a relationship growing up as I clearly had other priorities. Those around me assumed that I was serial dating because I liked to flirt and I always seemed to be surrounded by boys, but I wasn't. Surprisingly, my

[5] 1 Corinthians 13:4-5 "Love...does not look for its own interest."
[6] 1 Corinthians 10:34 "Let each one keep seeking, not his own advantage, but that of the other person."
[7] Psalm 26:4 "I avoid those who hide what they are."

first and proper relationship was when I was 18 years old. This boy was very patient in his pursuit of me and never stopped trying for over a year despite my many refusals. I did fancy him but I didn't need that kind of distraction as I was going through a lot emotionally at the time so we first built a healthy friendship and eventually, we started dating.

Because we had become good friends before dating and because we were hanging out with the same group of friends, we were always around each other and it was really nice. We genuinely enjoyed each other's company. He made me feel special and never forced or pressured me to do anything I didn't want to do. He was somehow different from the boys I knew. He was a couple of years older than me and quite mature for his age. Everything was good, too good until I started having doubts in mind due to my insecurities. I had never felt for anyone the way I was feeling for him so I broke up with him because in my mind I thought it was for the best. In my head it made perfect sense. My excuse was that I wasn't ready for a sexual relationship, though he never asked for it and never commented on it either, I just thought he may want it one day and it wouldn't be fair on him as I knew deep down I wasn't ready. The idea that one day I'll be having sex made me feel sick. The idea of being naked in front of someone else repulsed me which may have had something to do with what had happened to me in the past.

A couple of months after the break up, we tried again but I still felt like I was holding him back from something he could get from another girl. When I explained that to him, he made it clear that he wasn't with me for sex, "though it would be nice" he said "but sex isn't everything and it is not why I liked you in a first place." I was reassured and I knew he meant it. We were serious about each other, planning our future together etc. We often wondered about our future together etc. He was committed to make it work while I was busy self-sabotaging. and inevitably, because of my insecurities, I broke up with him again. I thought I didn't deserve a guy like him, he was too good to be true. My mind kept thinking "something is going to happen," and I didn't want him to break my heart, I was scared. My feelings for him were too overwhelming. I could see this was not a game for him as he continued to pursue me even after I broke his heart a second time. When I finally made up my mind to get back with him, he had moved on which broke my heart. Months later, he wanted to get back with me but I was moving to London. I did consider staying in Toulouse to be with him but I couldn't jeopardise my future like that. I think at that point we were both heartbroken.

Older but not wiser
In October 2003, I started my first job with a direct sales company which was my first job in London. I finally had English speaking friends and was living on my own in a hostel in Bayswater. I got on with a few work colleagues but was mostly friendly with one guy. I thought he was cool and genuine so we often went out with the rest of the team to hang out especially when we had a good day of sales in the office.

Though he didn't live far from work, he had a problem getting to work on time so we agreed that I would call him in the morning to wake him up and make sure he would get to work on time as he was on the verge of losing his job - those are the sort of things I would do for a friend.

One evening after work, we went to the pub to celebrate a very good day in the office with some other colleagues. Because it was quite late and no one was heading home in my direction, he suggested that I stay over at his place. I honestly didn't think anything of it because he never showed any romantic interest in me so I agreed. As this was a last minute arrangement, I had no spare clothes so he lent me a t-shirt to sleep with. He was living with his brother in Pimlico at the time so I had to share the bed with him, still didn't think anything of it.

I believe I was still very naive at that time as I didn't see anything wrong being at his place wearing a t-shirt and sleeping next to him after all he was my friend and never seemed to be interested in anything else with me. I had previously, and on a couple of occasions, slept next to male friends so to me this was no different. I also slept countless times next to my ex and nothing happened so why would anything happen now right!? My logic and assessment of the situation was very wrong.

In the early hours, I could feel him move closer to me but it was a cold night so I thought nothing of it and fell into a deep sleep. I am not sure how it happened as no words were spoken but I felt his heavy weight on top of me - I immediately startled from sleep and realised that he had started to penetrate me. I pushed him back and realised my knickers were pulled down so I started crying at the realisation that I had been violated. Though he didn't penetrate me fully, to me it didn't matter fully in or not, I had just lost my virginity! I was horrified. Though he kept apologising, I thought to myself, "This is it!". He tried to reassure me that he had not fully penetrated me yet I felt sore. I did not agree to that act nor gave him any indication that it was ok for him to proceed. I cried a lot that morning as I made my way back to the hostel. "What kind of sleep was I into that I didn't feel him pull my knickers down?" there was a gap in my memory I was unable to fill no matter how hard I tried. I sure wasn't intoxicated. I got in, showered and slept as it was now Saturday. I couldn't even tell my friends or my big sister what had happened, I was embarrassed, ashamed and aware that I would n't be able to answer some of the questions they may ask. I wasn't ready to have sex, let alone with him.

As a little girl, I always said that I would remain a virgin until I am married. It was so upsetting that I had to have a conversation with him. I didn't confront him about what had happened as I wanted to forget about it but I did tell him that we now needed to be in a relationship. It made perfect sense to me at the time as I didn't want to have to sleep with anybody else. My mind was all over the place yet he agreed which in this case revealed his primary intentions. We started our relationship a week after the incident and never referred to what got us together in the first place.

When the company relocated to Luton, some of our team followed and a couple of us agreed to rent a house there. I should have never gone there in the first place if I'm honest, this was my way out but I didn't see it. Even though we were to be in the same house, we chose to have our separate rooms. I liked him because we were friends but I didn't love him and I didn't think he did either. It was a big mistake though he proved himself to be a good and caring boyfriend, I was not in love with him and had no desire to be with him.

I can honestly say I knew nothing about sex and everything I knew was what he showed me. I didn't like the act, not because of him, but because I had no desire for it, so at times I would just lay there staring at the ceiling. It felt like a chore to me. The worse and careless part was that we were not even using any protection because he didn't like it and I didn't stop to question or impose it. I wasn't even on the pill!

What foolishness was this! We had a pregnancy scare towards the end of our relationship and from there on he became distant and I started having trust issues which led to us breaking up. Our relationship lasted over 6 months.

After the break up, I stayed single for a year as I had no desire to date or be in a relationship. My understanding of dating/relationship was that no one was out there dating or in a relationship without having sex and I didn't want to have sex anymore as I did not enjoy my first experience of it. This had also changed my views on boys and girls' friendships as I always thought it could be possible, but maybe it was less complicated when we are younger. I still have mixed feelings about it all.

A joke gone wrong
Late in the Summer 2005, I started dating a guy who happened to be the son of a family friend. He was lovely but my dad was definitely against that relationship. We went out for no longer than 2 months. Because I had the wrong idea of relationship and sex, we became physically involved very quickly. My thoughts, as mentioned above, were that no relationships couldn't happen without the element of sex so I reluctantly let it happen. We ended our relationship because of our parents constant nagging which became too much.

One day, one of his nosey friends saw me with a bloated tummy and assumed that I was pregnant, I did not contradict him. That evening, my ex called me and he sounded very annoyed with me. His choice of words was not very friendly as he proceeded to tell me that he did not want a baby, "I already have 2 children with 2 baby mama, what do you think my parents will think of me? I can't do this." he said. I kept quiet but because he was abusive, I stood my ground and didn't contradict the lie he heard and believed. When he hung up, I knew at that very instant, it was a very stupid thing to do and regretted it. I felt awful but at that time it made sense to get on his nerves. I went too far; I didn't think he took it seriously but a couple of days later he called me again about it. I told him to not worry because I was getting an abortion I had to make up one lie to cover another, that's how lies work. He said he wanted to see me so to make my lie believable, I booked an appointment at an abortion clinic and had received the letter as a proof to show him what I was about to "do". We met and he apologised about the way things were. That was my chance to come clean but I couldn't. I felt really bad but kept thinking of the repercussions of that lie because quite a few people were by then made aware of the situation. To him, I was pregnant with his baby, having an abortion and I kept it that way for years. In the next chapter I'll explain how this was dealt with.

Deception

I met my daughter's dad late in 2005. He was very charming, much older than me and we got on straight away. I met him through my little sister who was participating in an event he was organising at the time. During the event, I was drinking some alcohol during the event and as I had not eaten much that evening got very light headed (tipsy) quite quickly as a result. The agreement was that he would drive my sister home then take me home but because he was apparently too tired to drive from North London to West London he suggested that I stay over at his flat in East London. I should have really got off with my sister but he only informed me of his plan as we had already started driving away and were too far to turn around. I reluctantly agreed. We slept together that same evening and I ended up staying at his flat for a couple of days before he drove me back to my flat in West London. I had no idea where I was as I had never heard of Barking and when I looked outside I could only see buildings. I felt a bit stuck.

As we started our relationship, we did spend quite a lot of time together and though he was lovely there was something not right about him – I couldn't decipher what it was. he wasn't really open about his life; all I knew was that he had a daughter who lived in Switzerland but this information was only disclosed when I saw his phone's screensaver. He was quite self-centred and we were seeing each other on his terms. I got tired of the one way relationship so I stopped getting in touch and he did the same.

10th of May 2006 is the day when I found out I was pregnant. I actually didn't think I could be pregnant because a year before I was diagnosed with fibroids and the doctor told me that it would be very difficult for me to get pregnant. That Wednesday as I laid on the floor of my flat in pain, the last thing I was thinking about was pregnancy. After all I was on the pill though I slept with my ex without protection as I thought the pill was enough. That morning, I had an acute lower belly ache that pinned me to the floor and thought this could be due to the fibroids. The pain was excruciating, so I contacted the NHS[8] emergency line and was asked to attend an appointment at a nearby hospital, St Charles Hospital, in the following half hour from my call.

Without hesitation, I agreed to the appointment but I had to find the strength to pick myself up and make my way to the hospital. It took a lot of

---

[8] The English **National Health Service** (**NHS**) is one of the four publicly funded national healthcare systems in the United Kingdom (one for each constituent country). Some services, such as emergency treatment and treatment of infectious diseases, are free for everyone, including visitors

strength for me to get up, get ready and walk all the way to the hospital.

When it was finally my turn to see the doctor, I went in and explained my symptoms but also mentioned the fibroids findings in the past. The doctor asked me to get on the examining table then performed various tests including a feel of my abdomen which was obviously very tender and every push got me twisting in pain. He could not see what the problem was so he asked me for a urine sample as it would be the routine for abdominal pain to check for any infection.

As I was leaving, he remembered that he hadn't checked my urine sample so he did and guess what! I was pregnant. As soon as he said it, I burst into tears. I stood numb and clearly in shock. The doctor asked me to sit down and as we both sat down, I could see him looking at me feeling sorry but because he had to stay professional as he could not physically comfort me with a hug which is probably what I needed.

After a few minutes, I managed to calm myself down, the doctor got me some water and we got talking some more. Because of the pain and the fact that I was now confirmed to be pregnant, he referred me for a scan as he suspected that this could be an ectopic pregnancy[9]. The scan was booked at St. Mary's in Paddington. I left the doctor's office totally distraught and considering a number of scenarios obviously hoping that the test results were wrong.

As I walked to the bus stop, I called my big sister who was in Paris to tell her thinking she would be able to comfort me or at least reassure me. I couldn't stop crying so when she picked up the

---

[9] a pregnancy in which the foetus develops outside the uterus, typically in a fallopian tube.

phone she said, "Why are you crying like that?" I explained to her what had just happened and she exclaimed "Ah! You are crying as if someone died, you scared me!" I felt like she was being insensitive but according to her I shouldn't be crying like that because a child is a blessing. We talked for a while and she reassured me the best she could as I waited for the bus.

My bus journey to the hospital felt very long albeit it was 15 minutes. At a point I even wanted to get off the bus, run home and forget about it all. Upon arrival, they told me they were expecting me so my waiting time wasn't long at all. I was talked through the scan procedure and again explained what they were looking for.

The doctor explained the procedure once again when she entered the room and while doing the scan reassured me the pregnancy was in the right place. I was relieved but still in shock so on my way out I plucked up the courage to call my ex-boyfriend to tell him the news. To be honest, I wasn't sure about the way he would react but I still thought he needed to know. My worries were more to do with the fact that we had not spoken for a couple of weeks. When I told him the news, without hesitation he told me to have an abortion. His excuse was that we were not ready for this, which was true in a way but then he suggested that we could try again later, that must have been a joke right! I felt insulted by his reaction but thought he might be in shock and brushed it off.

I couldn't understand how people would happily lay down and have sex, whether protected or unprotected, but are somehow never ready for the consequences of it.

Though this was not one of my dreams or wish at such a young age, I wasn't prepared to have an abortion to accommodate him. Even though I was not a proper Christian, I did not believe in abortion and vowed to never do it myself. I would never judge anyone who would do that or thought about it but it was simply not something I was prepared to go through. At the time, when I told him I would not have an abortion, I felt bad because I didn't want him to think that I wanted to keep the baby to trick him into anything. I understood we were done, we were clearly not together when I found out I was pregnant so how could he even suggested that we could try again later, that was beyond me. Were both decisions selfish? Was he being selfish or was I being selfish?

Once the scan report was printed and handed to me, I was sent home with painkillers to alleviate the pain. I was thankful to God that the pregnancy was in the right place, which meant the pain would eventually settle itself though I still had excruciating pain and cramps for a couple of weeks after my hospital visit.

In London, the only person who was aware of this pregnancy, apart from my ex, was one of my little sisters as I was still thinking of a way to break this news down to my dad. I could not stay away from my dad for a very long time as they were used to seeing me at least once a week because I worked so close to their home. I decided to pay them a visit a couple of days after finding out I was pregnant. That afternoon, I was in severe pain, curled up and started to cry as it was unbearable. My little sister was worried and called my stepmum. At that moment, I thought I had no choice but to tell her the truth which she promised to keep to herself until we could find a good time to tell my dad. I was relieved by her reaction and the fact that I had found an ally.

The day before my 23rd birthday, my dad found out the news through the grapevine who happened to be my uncle who himself heard it through the grapevine[10]. This had taught me the potential of Chinese whispers[11] and gossip in destroying someone's reputation. I was very annoyed as no one bothered checking the facts or the truth with me. I stood accused of what seemed to be the crime of the century. What was even more shocking was that the rumour was that not only I was pregnant but that I also had HIV and was sleeping around. I seethed with anger.

At that time, my life was mostly spent between work, home, my parents' and church. I would never have met my ex-boyfriend if I had never accompanied my little sister to the event.

My ex-boyfriend was known to my dad because he needed his permission for my little sister to take part in his event so naturally my dad had no problem calling him in for a meeting that evening.

When he arrived, my sister escorted him to the living room where I sat in their presence like a naughty little girl. He looked pretty relaxed and took a seat not far from me. My dad proceeded to ask him some questions and one of them was "What do you think Paulette should do? Are you going to take care of that baby?" Again without hesitation, my ex reiterated to all present, dad, stepmun and myself, what he had told me earlier that week - to have an abortion. Then he said that he had heard that I was sleeping around therefore this could also not be his child. My stepmun flew in a rage seeing how careless and immature he was with his words. She had every right to be

---

[10] To hear something through unofficial means, often through word-of-mouth gossip. This idiom is a popular expression used throughout the English-speaking world to refer to unsubstantiated information that is passed between people who are not directly in connection with the source.

[11] a game in which a message is distorted by being passed around in a whisper.

angry but there was no reaction or emotions coming from my dad. I was very upset therefore chose not to speak unless spoken to because I wanted the meeting to end as quickly as possible.

To my surprise, he explained his reasons for not wanting the baby and this was because he was married. I was beside myself. As previously stated, I knew he had a daughter who lived in Switzerland but never knew he was married as I stayed with him for many days at a time and no sign of a woman living in his flat. To me, that was another knife in the back. I felt sick at the idea that I had been sleeping with a married man. I wasn't, and still am not, the type of woman who goes after someone else's man!

Anyway, he didn't take that meeting seriously because as soon as he left and got home he called me asking what my dad said after he left but his tone of voice was indifferent as if this was a joke to him. I felt he disrespected not only me but my dad too.

The most illogical decision I made was that out of fear of being pregnant and alone, I got back with him. Yes, even after the meeting and all I found out, I went back to him. Because his supposedly wife was in Switzerland, he had the privilege to live a double life and I went along with his charade. Rest assured this did not last very long because I eventually got back to my senses as I started seeing things in him that made me question myself and the future of whatever we were. I was kidding myself, this was not the relationship I had hoped for or was destined for. He definitely wasn't going to take his responsibility seriously and I somehow felt backed into a corner.

For someone who was supposedly married, his behaviour with me was very possessive and he sometimes felt as if I was his child in the way he would speak to me. One day, he got told off by one of his friends for the way he was talking to me not only because it wasn't nice but also because it was done in the presence of others. I recall him being a bit controlling as one day I was at church and wanted to have a chat with one of the ladies I really liked and considered a mother figure. I wanted to tell her the news before she heard it elsewhere. As I was talking to her, my phone rang and it was him. I had left his house that morning to go to church and I think he was expecting me to be back straight after the service for some reason. I explained to him that I was talking to a few friends after church and that we were thinking about going to the park as the weather was nice. He started shouting at me and ordered me to get home. The lady I was talking to, who was sitting right next to me, could hear him shouting. He then gave me an hour to get home. The lady was looking at me completely baffled. When I hung up, she asked me if it was him then she shook her head in disbelief. I told her what he said though she seemed to have heard quite a lot. She was upset about the whole situation but also the fact that he thought it was okay for him to speak to me in that manner and also impose curfews. Nevertheless, we continued our conversation then she hugged me and asked me if I was ok, even though I wasn't I said that I was. On the tube, I became so anxious as I felt like a child who stayed out past her curfew. When I got to his place, he was busy watching TV. He didn't have anything to say to me and neither did I so I took refuge in the bedroom.

On another occasion, I remember being really sick at work so I called him to pick me up and take me home. I had a very high temperature and was diagnosed with a urinary tract infection the day before. When he picked me up, he took me to his place though I had asked him to take me to my place as I knew I wouldn't be able to rest at his. As he was driving, I had no choice but to go where he was taking me. Once indoors, I crashed in bed as I was so poorly and stayed there until the next day. The next day, he woke me up asking me to make him breakfast. I was still quite unwell so I told him to make it himself but he insisted that I should get up and make his breakfast. I turned around and asked "If I was ill would you just leave it to me to take care of the baby." His response was pretty disturbing as he calmly answered "Yes, you wanted to keep it." Then he jumped out of bed and went to the shower. I think he was still expecting me to make him breakfast but as he closed the shower door, I got out of bed, quickly put my clothes on and left. I had tolerated enough and this was the last straw for me. The infection has weakened me and I looked like a zombie dragging myself through the streets of Barking looking for the nearest tube station, my only desire was to make it home safely. During the journey home, which was under an hour, my mind kept replaying what had happened as I couldn't believe what I had heard. I was saddened and shocked by the turn of events. That day was the last time I saw him. He didn't bother calling me and I did the same, maybe he did me a favour.

Sometimes it takes a particular incident or your personal trigger to push you to do better or escape from pain, abuse and/or hurt. That was the case for me that day, I felt like I had no other option than to run for my life with every bit of sanity I had left.

Faith tested
Since the meeting, my dad had stopped talking to me. I knew he was disappointed but I didn't expect him to cut me off like that! He forbade my sisters to speak or hang out with me so I was completely isolated during most of my pregnancy.

But things didn't quite end there because rumours kept going around and coming back to me. I was heartbroken.

One day, I even received an anonymous threat letter which I had to take to the police. I never thought in a million years I would have been going through something so heartbreaking at a young age. I wasn't prepared for this and felt unsafe at home so I went to live with the lady from church I mentioned earlier for a couple of months before staying with a friend from church for a while.

At church, I finally plucked up the courage to tell our lady pastor. With what had already happened with my dad, it wasn't easy at all telling her and her reaction was definitely not what I expected. The words she had for me were very harsh and cut deep in my soul. On that day I left the church thinking that I was worthless, that God wouldn't love anyone like me. I was crushed even more as her words stuck in my mind and gave me sleepless nights. I no longer wanted to attend church.

That summer, I went on holiday in Toulouse to visit my family but also to break the news. My pregnancy bump had already started to show so there would have been no way for me to hide this during my entire stay. I told my aunt who was disappointed but still understood my decision to keep it after I had told her the whole story.

During my stay, my aunt was against the idea of me visiting my great uncle; I guess she knew what his reaction would be but I still wanted to go as my big sister and niece were there.

Whilst there, I became very anxious and hid my bump as best as I could by staying in the bedroom most of the time but because this was unlike me it became quite obvious that I was up to something. One day as I was walking out of the kitchen through the living room to get back to the bedroom, my great uncle asked to have a word. I became very anxious as I took a seat. Of course, he had noticed my growing bump and went on to say how disappointed he was. Sadly, his choice of words were not encouraging nor loving. His words were very harsh because of the fact that my big sister was already a single mother, his own daughter just had a baby at a very young age and his niece also had a child and was in a complicated relationship. His anger was due to the fact that they had high hopes for me. I was considered the brain of the family and was now a disappointment. His exact words were "Do you think because others have had the grace to marry, you would have the same grace to?." I couldn't believe what I had heard and my big sister who was present at that time was furious with him. I listened to him as he went on and on about the shame this has brought to the family. I kept quiet, took it all in and left the next day.

I was made redundant that summer so understandably my mind was all over the place. When I got back to London, I looked for work although my bump was showing, I still managed to secure a full-time job with Specsavers as an Optical Advisor/Receptionist. After starting my job, I had to let my manager know that I was pregnant and apologised for not mentioning it at the interview. To my surprise, she was also expecting and was very understanding.

During my pregnancy, my stepmum would visit me from time to time at home or we would meet by the tube station. She was working in the area and always made sure to check on me. I don't even think my dad was aware of our meetings of which he probably would have disapproved.

My pregnancy wasn't a great journey to start with and it went from bad to worse. I carried the feeling of shame throughout my pregnancy and had no one to turn to it seemed. I felt like I had left everyone down from my family to the church to some of my friends. Having to deal with all this on my own, my health deteriorated from having sciatica[12] to pre-eclampsia[13] Because of my health issues, I was rehoused from my flat to a mother and baby unit in Notting Hill Gate.

It's early days
My due date was early January 2007 so I worked from the end of September until early December 2006 then started my maternity leave. A couple of days after my work ended, I was admitted to hospital because of pre-eclampsia and the risk to the baby. It looked like they were ready to deliver the baby earlier than January.

On Friday 15th December 2006, after a review of my medical notes, the doctors had decided to do a scan on Monday and induce me. I had to be mentally prepared for this as I didn't want to be induced. Again, as usual practice, the procedure was explained and I realised I had no choice because the baby and I were at risk. I had to hear this news on my own and make sense of everything.

That Sunday, 17th December, I remember not being able to lie down in bed because it felt really uncomfortable. There was no pain but clear discomfort. I told the night nurse who told me she could not give me more medicine as I had had all the medicine that was prescribed to me that day, so she advised me to try to sleep in a different

---

[12] Sciatica is when the sciatic nerve, which runs from your hips to your feet, is irritated. It usually gets better in 4 to 6 weeks but can last longer.
[13] a condition in pregnancy characterized by high blood pressure, sometimes with fluid retention and proteinuria.

position or walk for a bit. I walked up and down the labour ward corridor the whole night until morning came.

That Monday morning at 8.30am, when the doctors came to do the morning checks after the handover from the night staff, they examined me and told me that I was fully dilated and would give birth that morning. From there, I was rushed to a delivery room. I was all alone in the hospital at that time and although it didn't show, I was panicking on the inside. I only had a few minutes to make the necessary phone calls while they were getting ready. All I kept thinking was "I'm not even ready to give birth! How can I be giving birth I don't even have any contractions!? My hospital bag is at home; I have no clothes for the baby."

By the time the nurses settled me in the delivery room, 2 of my friends arrived and I felt a bit more relaxed. The doctors and nurses were discussing anaesthetics and thought that maybe I'll need a C-section. My water didn't break so one of the nurses had to break it and from then on it all went very quickly. There was no time for an epidural, not that I wanted one, and I tried gas and air but I couldn't understand how it works so ended up not taking any pain relief. I had no contractions all the way through and gave birth like that. The nurse broke my water around 9.30am and my daughter was born at 11.23am on Monday 18th December 2006. I knew it was a girl and had already chosen a name for her. I named her after my mum and my grandmother so she had an original double barrel name.

The joy of seeing her outweighed the pain I had been through during my entire pregnancy. I was over the moon but I think I zoned out because when I came back around, there were noises and a lot of agitation around me. The doctors seemed panicked and were asking my friends to leave the room. I asked what was happening and the nurse explained that I was losing too much blood and they were not able to stop it. They didn't know where it was coming from either. My daughter was taken out of my arms to the back of the room where I could see her. The nurse started pressing on my belly and I could feel the warm blood gushing out. They then found a tear and needed to quickly start sewing, though this was not the reason for the blood loss but it would help them see. The anaesthesia administered to that area didn't work so I felt every ins, outs and pulls of that needle stitch. After a while, it all settled and my friends were allowed back in along with my stepmum and her sister who had arrived while all this was happening.

Doctors and nurses who were not part of my delivery process, kept coming in to congratulate me as they said it was the quietest birth ever. To me it was normal, I just did what I was asked to do and I didn't think screaming would help much so I kept quiet and pushed.

My daughter was a healthy weight despite the risk of low birth weight due to the pre-eclampsia, she was absolutely fine. I loved her the minute I saw her; it was a kind of love I never felt before. Me and her had been through a lot. We were not discharged from the hospital straight away as we had to stay a bit longer because I needed to have a blood transfusion. Apparently I had lost nearly 1L of blood during the delivery process.

To my surprise, my dad, who I had not spoken to during most of my pregnancy, came to visit in hospital with my stepmum. At first it was awkward as we did not have much to say to each other, then we just made small conversation. My dad commented that my daughter looked like her dad which I couldn't deny. Things were clearly different having not spoken for months but I was willing to give it a go. "Where do we go from here?", I thought to myself. I needed my dad and he had rejected me because I was pregnant. For someone who wanted to build bridges he sure burned a few by abandoning me in that hour of need. We chatted for a bit then they left.

For me, Single motherhood started the minute I got pregnant I guess though everything sank in when I made my way home from the hospital by cab holding my little baby. We were alone. There was no welcome home party for us except for the staff at the mother and baby unit who made sure we settled properly that afternoon. The fact that it was Christmas the following week didn't help the way I was feeling. I was on my own and despite the fact that I was tired from it all, I had to go out that same day to buy extra things for my daughter because she was a "tiny baby" and all the clothes I had bought were too big for her.

Our life together started from that moment. I registered the birth on my own and I did feel uncomfortable sitting in the waiting area with those happy couples. It felt like a punishment. It may have all been in my head but I felt the judgemental looks I got especially when I was asked about the father. I felt like telling the administrator "the father has denied the pregnancy and moved on with his life".

I cannot hide that the beginning of single motherhood was emotionally hard but the fact that she was such a content baby made it slightly easier on both of us. She was a very good baby.

Getting by
After a while, things with my family started to get a bit better.

At church, I had a problem forgiving the pastor for what she had said so it took me a while to start going there again though she visited me at the hospital I was still hurt. I couldn't understand how someone in her position could be so cruel with their words.

In March 2007, I started attending church again though not as regularly as I used to because my heart wasn't there anymore, especially when I saw how they treated couples who had babies just after me. I felt like the black sheep because I wasn't married so I didn't deserve the "special treatments" and fuss others were getting. I had been demoted from teaching in the children's ministry as soon as they found out I was pregnant. To me, most of them were just a bunch of hypocrites and I couldn't stand being around them. I left the church deeply hurt. Yes, I admit I was bitter over this.

I was churchless for a little while but didn't forget about God. Though I struggled to see his love for me, everything around me reminded me of His goodness. My daughter was healthy and thriving and I was alive to see that.

Late August 2010, I started attending church again but the main church this time. I thought it would be easier for me to be around people who didn't know me or my history, I needed a fresh start. I call it the main church because Kensington Temple LCC has many satellite churches and the church I was going to before is one of those satellites. I felt at peace attending though I wasn't committed but at least I was fellowshipping again.

Short lived celibate
I started dating again when my daughter was just over a year old. The general rule was: no man around my daughter unless it turned out to be a serious relationship.

A couple of months before meeting my son's dad, I had made the decision to celibate. I was happy with my life being just the way it was. I had a couple of dates here and there as mentioned but they didn't end up the way I wished they would so I wanted a break from the dating scene, I had no desire for a boyfriend in that season of my life but then I met my son's dad in September 2010.

Passing red flags for greens
I met him one evening as I was going to a party with one of my exes (yes, I had remained very good friends with a couple of my exes). I was unsure about going to that party in the first place but my friend, who was visiting from France, insisted that we should go out that evening. Looking back, I should have listened to my gut feeling.

We journeyed to the party by bus as I was not driving at the time. As we were waiting for our second bus, a guy I knew was with him and we greeted each other and as it happened they were going to that same party! I moved back to see who he was with and I could see him looking at me and remember thinking "Wow, this guy is really handsome!".

Please allow me to insist on the fact that being handsome or having good looks doesn't pay the bills and it shouldn't be your main criteria in choosing a partner!

During the party, we kept looking at each other until he finally approached and asked for a dance. While we were dancing, we talked and he made his interest known. I wasn't sure at first but I was certainly flattered. When the music ended, I went my way and bumped into one of my male friends who asked me to dance. I went along and as we were dancing he kept mentioning the way the other guy, my son's dad, was staring at me. I felt a bit uncomfortable as it looked like one of those jealous boyfriends. There was something dark in his look that made me feel uncomfortable. My friend kept asking if he was my boyfriend as he couldn't understand why he was looking at me that way. After the song we were dancing to ended, I walked back to my table and he came over asking that we have a chat outside. I followed him outside, we chatted and laughed before exchanging numbers. I didn't think he would call me to be honest.

From our first encounter things moved on rather quickly. At the time, he was very pleasant – a real charmer. He called me the day after we met and we arranged to see each other face to face again. I remember being at work looking at the time and getting really nervous as I kept thinking "Maybe if he sees me again he may not like what he sees". I got on the phone to a good friend of mine at the time and she reassured me all the way there. I made a stop and bought 2 pairs of shoes I really didn't need but that was my way of coping with the stress.

What made it worse was that he asked me to meet him at his place which was where he lived with his mum and siblings. I was quite surprised that his mum would allow him to bring a girl home as no African mum would allow that, or maybe it was just the ones I knew.

This relationship felt different as we used to spend hours on the phone, he was very present unlike what I had experienced before. My idea at the time was that I didn't want to date here and there so to have a start like this was very encouraging. I wanted to build a proper relationship and not quit at the first sign of trouble like I did in my previous relationships.

I remember him walking through the snow one night to see me because I was ill. He came in helped me to bed, staying until I fell asleep and left; that melted my heart. Surely, he was the one I thought as he seemed to like everything about me and I liked him too.

Having standards

Dating in the past, I had very little patience towards what I considered as unacceptable behaviour (i.e. no calls answered for 2 days, you're out), therefore, I did not have any long term relationships so I thought this time I owed to do it differently. So guess what!? I lowered my standards, I thought I was being too fussy and no man could actually meet my standards and if I kept them that high I was at risk of being all alone.

When we first met, he told me he was 2 years younger than me but he lied about that and even when he told me his real age a couple of weeks later, I said to myself, "Ok, I can overlook this detail as long as he treats me right". He was in fact 5 years younger than me! Then I stupidly remembered that famous saying "Age ain't nothing but a number", I had never dated someone younger than me and I didn't think it was a good excuse to break up with him.

I remember one night, a couple of weeks into the relationship, as I was getting ready to go out with him that evening, he messaged me over Facebook messenger accusing me of giving him chlamydia[14]. I was shocked and appalled by the rudeness and tone of his messages. Luckily for me, I had done a test around the same time and my results were negative so he had no leg to stand on. The truth quickly surfaced that he had in

---

[14] **Chlamydia** is a sexually transmitted infection caused by the bacterium **Chlamydia** trachomatis. It's passed from person to person through sex, and it can cause a wide variety of complications if it's not treated.

fact been sleeping with me and another girl at the time, and she was the one who gave it to him he claimed or he could have given it to her, but that was for them to agree. I couldn't believe the immaturity of his messages so we ended things there. I felt so disrespected.

After a couple of weeks, I contacted him to get my friend's DVD I lent him as she wanted it back. I forgot he had it and was not too pleased that I now had to see his face again but I had no choice. When I got to his place and evening after work, we chatted in front of the door as I had no intentions to go in. Despite what he had said and done, I was completely smitten. I couldn't resist him and didn't try hard to so without any words being said, we were back together that evening. He did apologise for what he had said and the apology seemed genuine so I thought to myself, "Is this a good enough reason to break up?" (It was! BIG RED FLAG). Unconsciously, I was settling and my standards were once again lowered.

When it all started
I vividly remember the first time he laid his hands on me like it was yesterday. I never thought in a million years this would ever happen to me. It happened earlier on in the relationship, I believe it was in November 2010, we were play-fighting one evening in my living room but what started as a game, he initiated, quickly turned into something vicious. During what I thought was part of the play fight, he threw me on the sofa and had me in a position where my nails accidentally scratched him. He jumped up and as he let go of me, he punched me in the back, not full force but hard enough for me to feel the ache of the punch. I turned around and when I saw the look on his face, I knew that this wasn't done in a playful way. I didn't mean to scratch him. I was really upset and I ran to my bedroom to gather myself and sat

in silence trying to process what had just happened.

He took some time to come to the bedroom but he eventually did. He apologised because he realised how upset I was though I'm not sure he really meant it as he pushed the blame on me saying, "You shouldn't have done that". I let that one slide. He made me believe that I shouldn't have reacted the way I did. Was my reaction over the top? This was the beginning of reverse psychology, another big red flag. This is what you would call gaslighting[15] which was typical of him.

Growing up I've always told myself that if a man puts his hands on me the relationship would be over. Believe me this is easier said than done especially when emotions / feelings are involved and you will see what I mean by that.

What you see is what you get
I'll be honest here, I could clearly see that he wasn't as committed as I was to this relationship yet I hoped he would eventually be hence why I did everything I could to please him. I was in love with his potential as I could see who he could be. I'd be very careful falling in love with a man's potential especially if he is not willing to exploit or aware of it himself.

He had moments when he was good but it was really and truly on his own terms. He would come and go. Break up and come back. That's what you would call emotional abuse but I didn't see it that way. I must have been crazy because I was still thinking that we could make it work, that I should not give up so easily. And you hear people say "relationships go through this phase", "it's early days, things will change"; and then "there's

---

[15] to manipulate (someone) by psychological means into doubting their own sanity.

better and there's worse, but you don't want to leave him and find yourself with worse". So there I was thinking and praying "he'll change, surely he'll change".

I thought my love would change him. Wrong, wrong, wrong! Let me tell you that a man only changes if he wants to, not because you stick around and allow all the nonsense to carry on, not because you love him but because he loves you. Bottom line is, he has to do it for himself, see the benefit of changing for himself.

He cheated countless times and even came home in the early days with love bites on his neck and his excuse was "My female friend just wanted to know how it looks" but of course she wasn't his girlfriend, so I shouldn't be upset about it. He really thought I was a fool but then again I showed him no better by sticking around.

From visiting to moving in
Just like that and I'm not even sure how, we found ourselves living together from him staying over from time to time to him being there full time, it just happened! For him it was very convenient I guess because he was living at home with his mum so living with me meant unlimited freedom and no questions asked.

At first, I liked having him around but then I quickly was not convinced that this was best for me or my daughter. It happened too quickly and his presence felt like a weight. Because he wasn't working, he spent most of his days at home listening to music loudly or watching TV and at times, I felt like he was taking over our space. Even imposing my daughter to call him "dad", though her dad wasn't present she had a dad so I was not comfortable with that idea but my daughter being so young went along. We argued back and forth about this and I stated to him "don't make her call you dad if you know you are not prepared to be one for her in every way." I knew he cared about her but I wasn't sure how much of a father figure he would be at that stage because of his inconsistency with me.

He was very inconsistent and very up and down with his mood too. In April 2011, on a Saturday to be precise, my daughter was at my sister's house for the weekend, he came home with yet another love bite on his neck and while I was questioning him, he distracted me by asking to see my phone. I can't remember what I was doing on my phone, though I think I was on Facebook, but he snatched it off my hand. I really didn't mind him going through my phone because I had nothing to hide but I didn't like how he got hold of it and the reason behind his demand. Nevertheless, I wasn't about to wrestle with him. Because my phone turned off in his hand while we were arguing about what he had just done, he ordered me to enter my PIN. As he was going through my phone searching for whatever he thought he could find, I thought "Ok, since you're going through my phone, let me go through yours then". His phone was by the couch armrest so I grabbed it, and even though I didn't know his PIN, he flew into a rage.

At first, I thought he was joking so I ran into the bedroom and hid the phone by the window sill. Now, you may stop to think "Why didn't you just give him his phone back!" and yes I could have but hold on, what gives him the right to go through my phone and me not to go through his? This didn't seem fair. He got very angry and in a way I had never seen or experienced before. As he entered the bedroom, I noticed the change in his face and body language, and became really scared though I refused to show it. As he paced towards me, he grabbed me by the throat and pinned me against the wardrobe. I couldn't breathe, I seriously couldn't breathe. I became numb as he swung me across the room from the wardrobe onto the bed, still holding my throat. I felt like a ragdoll. Every time he would pin me on the wardrobe, my head would hit the mirrors there. If evil had a face, I was staring right at it as he looked possessed doing what he was doing.

He took my head and banged it many times on the mirror and all I was thinking was "He's going to kill me". During that episode all that mattered to him was his phone, as he shouted "Where is my f@#$ing phone!".

He was shouting in my face. How could I even answer with his hands around my throat? Nothing made sense at that point. This episode, though brief in itself, felt like it was never going to end. When he finally let go of my throat, I was able to tell him where his phone was.

When he got his phone, I ran and locked myself in the bathroom. I felt like disappearing. I felt so small and stupid. My throat, my head and my back were hurting and all I could do was cry. I looked at myself in the mirror then sat on the bathroom floor crying, feeling sorry for myself. A thought crossed my mind that he would follow me there to carry on his attack so I sat with my back against the closed door. "How could he?" I thought. I was in shock and to make matters worse my little sister was on her way to my place as we were going shopping that afternoon.

Shortly after, he came knocking on the bathroom door and begged me to let him in. He sounded genuinely upset as if he had been crying too. I waited a bit to gather myself and my thoughts then I eventually opened the door slightly, just enough to see. He looked normal, he looked like himself again so innocent. He apologised profusely but I didn't want to let him come near me. He promised it would never happen again, that this was the first and last time. He looked so remorseful I chose to believe him and my decision was based on my feelings for him, nothing else. As per what he said, he had never hit a woman before but I later on found out that he did hit one of his exes and that was the reason they broke up.

After that, things calmed down for a while though he was still inconsistent and mean at times, I focused on the good times. Even though he didn't hit me anymore, what he did to me at times was inhuman but then again by staying with him I showed him that I didn't deserve any better.

I recall several incidents when he came home in the early morning hours from his weekend DJ job, dragged me out of bed by my feet to make him food and made me sit with him whilst he ate. He didn't care whether it was 3am and I had to be up to get to work as long as he got what he wanted. He made me sit with him while he was eating because he didn't want to eat alone. Imagine making fufu[16] at 3am with sleepy arms, I felt like his slave more than his girlfriend. If I didn't do things the way he asked, he would stop talking to me for days at a time, that was my punishment. Those silent treatments were very random and unnecessary.

From then on, his behaviour was more aggressive. Everything I did, from what I wore and ate to who I was hanging out with became a problem for him. The things he once loved about me became the very things that annoyed him.

---

[16] dough made from boiled and ground plantain or cassava, used as a staple food in parts of West and Central Africa. Other flours, such as semolina, maize flour or mashed plantains may take the place of cassava flour.

Then he started calling me names such as fat or commenting on my skin complexion.

He knew how to hit me with hurtful one-liners such as "You'll end up like your sister and your mother," using what I had told him about my past against me. His goal was to lower my self-esteem so that he can increase his own, because it made him feel powerful. It worked.

The fact that he got a reaction out of me reinforced his behaviour and actions. My reactions taught him that he had the power to affect my emotional state. He caused me to doubt myself. I no longer felt like the person I used to be.

Cheated on
From what I know, he cheated on me more than 5 times if not 10 but I was made aware of a few of his trysts. The moments he cheated were not one offs because he actually got into a relationship with some of those girls. When questioned, he would always deny it and become very aggressive. Being cheated on made me feel worthless and unwanted. On some occasions, when exposed, he would compare me to those girls which left me feeling even worse. He would speak of them as if I was no match for their beauty and skills. I questioned myself to the point where I started losing my confidence, I tried changing myself to meet his desires but that wasn't enough.

We are pregnant!
After just a year of being together, I got pregnant and because at that time we were "at peace", it was good news to us. We had talked about eventually having children but I didn't expect it to happen so soon as I was still unsure about his commitment. I had reluctantly agreed to have my Mirena coil[17] removed a couple of months prior to

being pregnant. After getting the news, we started making plans and all seemed well. I found out I was pregnant when I went for a sexual health check up at St Mary's and along with the news of pregnancy I was also told that I had chlamydia. I couldn't believe it! This was proof that he was still sleeping around but I overlooked it for the sake of the baby I was carrying. I had it all wrong.

I didn't want to be alone through another pregnancy and become a single mother again, he knew that. I was really annoyed with him but I kept quiet after reporting what the doctor said. He didn't argue with me this time as he also got tested and was positive. We were both treated but I was very anxious about taking such treatment though the nurse reassured me that it would not affect the development of the foetus in any way.

We shared the news with his mum who was pleased though the look on her face somehow not in line with what she was saying. I didn't know how to tell my dad but because of my growing bump, I decided to announce the news as soon as possible. My ex supported that decision so we set up a day to go and visit my family. I had never introduced a man to my dad, or any adults in my family, so this was quite stressful to begin with and it didn't get any better as the day of our visit drew closer. then what was meant to be a nice visit turned into my dad interrogating my ex. Now, at first I was annoyed but this revealed quite a lot at the time which I again chose to completely ignore.

My dad asked questions any dad would ask but he was not convinced by the sincerity of his answers and found him to be immature. His answers were very vague and carried some

[17] A Mirena coil is a hormone-releasing IUD (intrauterine device) that is over 99% effective at preventing pregnancy for as long as you want, for up to 5 years.

uncertainties. Example, my dad asked, "What are your plans for both of you in the future", his answer was "We'll see".

As the evening went on my dad seemed more and more irritated and I started feeling uncomfortable. I wanted to leave so we left straight after dinner. The walk to the car was very silent and awkward. I was thinking about what I heard and he was too. As we got in the car, he started venting about what had happened and was very annoyed at the fact that my dad questioned him in such a manner. I couldn't quite understand the basis for his annoyance, his answers were simply incoherent with someone who is in a relationship and about to become a father. He was adamant that my dad was trying to pressure him into something.

Going through a miscarriage

On Sunday 2nd October 2011, when he had gone to his DJ work, I was at home when I had a strange feeling about the baby in the middle of the night so I called him. I wasn't bleeding nor did I have any pain, I just had a strange feeling. It may have been hard for him to take me seriously because I had no symptoms so he didn't come home until the following morning at his usual time. To be honest, I knew deep down he wasn't going to leave that party to come home as I was never a priority to him, everything else came before me and I sadly got used to it.

That Monday morning, after dropping off my daughter to school, I asked him to accompany me to the hospital because I still had that gut feeling that something was wrong with the baby. The bus journey to the hospital was very silent. When we got there, the wait for the scan felt like an eternity.

The scan room was very silent as the doctor proceeded to scan my abdomen. It only took him a few minutes to realise that there was no heartbeat. He checked a few times but nothing. I think I zoned out when he told us that the baby had no heartbeat. I had scans prior to that and was always able to hear the baby's heartbeat! I miscarried at 22 weeks.

The doctor talked me through my options which were: taking a pill to speed up the process of having the termination of pregnancy (just like an abortion) or to wait for mother nature to do her work as my body would naturally reject the foetus but that would take some time. I didn't know what to do and at that point I just wanted to go home so I asked the doctor to give me a couple of days to think about it all.

On our way home, I could see he was as upset as I was but we were both not in a talking mood. Many thoughts rushed through my head as I cried all the way home. I did wonder if the chlamydia was a cause for the miscarriage.

When we got home, I went straight to bed, I just wanted to sleep and forget everything. I kept crying while touching my belly. This was the first time I had to mourn someone I would never meet. He called his mum who came over that evening and I was very grateful as my stepmum and dad couldn't.

The next day when we chatted, he blamed himself for giving me chlamydia and assumed I was blaming him too but I didn't, my mind was elsewhere. I kept thinking there is a lifeless baby inside of me and I had a decision to make.

On Wednesday 5th October 2011, I still hadn't made up my mind but that morning I started having severe tummy pains, so bad that I had to see my GP as an emergency appointment. The doctor gave me some strong painkillers which I could not take until I had eaten. Before going home, I decided to go do some shopping nearby. As I walked through the shop's aisles, I felt a sudden gushing down of warm liquid down my trousers. It felt like something popped. Instinctively, I knew what it was. I managed to get to the till and pay for my shopping but I could still feel the warm flow. When I got home, I took my trousers off and I was soaked in blood. We both panicked. He suggested that we call the hospital but for some reason I wasn't ready to go to the hospital, I wasn't ready for my baby to be out yet, so we argued back and forth. We finally agreed that I would have a shower and wait for my daughter's school pick up time so we could drop her off at his mum and go to the hospital. The bleeding was on and off from the moment I came out of the shower, but I knew I could not stay home. My heart was breaking thinking about what was happening inside of me.

I felt really tired so I laid on the couch in the living room to rest as he watched TV. As time passed, it was now school pick up time so he got ready to go. By the time he got to the door, I was on the toilet with the door open as we were discussing what we were doing. As I had finished peeing and was getting ready to wipe myself, I suddenly felt a mass pass, it was the foetus passing and I heard it drop in the toilet. I quickly jumped up the toilet seat. I heard him ask me what was wrong just before passing out in his arms. Lucky for me he was standing by the toilet door otherwise it would have been a very bad fall. I had never fainted before.

When I regained consciousness, I was in the bedroom. My upper body was on the bed and my legs were hanging down. I could hear him on the phone shouting at the ambulance services. When I looked down, I noticed he had changed what I was wearing at the bottom, I may have continued bleeding and didn't have a chance to put my underwear back on. I was wearing one of his basketball shorts with my UGG boots, what a sight!

When the ambulance crew finally arrived, they checked me over. One of them went to the toilet to check if they could see the foetus but the toilet had already been flushed. "My baby was flushed away", I thought as I closed my eyes to pray for strength to get through this. By the time I was wheeled to the ambulance waiting downstairs, his brother had already picked up my daughter from school to take her to his mum's. All I could do was cry as I was so sad but relieved that I didn't have to take any medicine and/or have the foetus surgically removed by vacuum aspiration. I was traumatised by what I had felt when the foetus passed through into the toilet, I couldn't stop thinking about it.

When we arrived at the hospital, I was escorted for a scan straight away as they wanted to see whether or not there was any residue of the foetus left in the uterus; and there was. I stayed 3 days in hospital as I needed to have a small procedure to remove the residue.

They removed what was left on the 2nd day of my stay. This was done without anaesthetics as they introduced a long surgical tool[18] to pull it out. I closed my eyes as I felt every pull and wanted to scream. For something they called tiny, it sure felt like it was big enough to create cramping pain with every pull as the tool gently pulled it out.

During my time at the hospital, he really stepped up as a partner and a father. He was taking my daughter to school every day, then coming to the hospital, picking her up from school to take her to

---

[18] Hemostats clamp.

his mum, to then come back to the hospital to stay with me until visiting hours were over. To me this was one of our good times when I really saw his kindness and love shine through.

Back to square one

When I got home from the hospital, to my surprise, the house was a mess. I was upset but then I thought he had done so much over the past couple of days that I should just be grateful that he stuck around and did what he did. In my head, I made it seem like he did me a favour instead of seeing this as a normal partnership. I was so grateful that I didn't want to upset him by making any comment.

So I was out of my hospital bed and back to washing plates and cleaning around before I got myself settled. Life as I knew it started again and he was already off on a trip to France with his DJ crew. He didn't think twice when the opportunity presented itself even though I needed rest and maybe just maybe I needed him to take care of me for a change. I'm not sure if that was his way of dealing with what had happened, as in mourning, but he was distant and it didn't take long before he went back to concentrating on himself with no care for me or my daughter.

He never was a big helper around the house like a proper partner would, whether physically or financially, I barely got any help from him. One of his excuses was that it was MY job and I never said thank you when he did clean! When he first said that to me, I thought he was joking because if we lived together so why should I thank him for cleaning a space that we both share! I'm not saying that I wasn't grateful but the way he went on and on about it was unreasonable. On most occasions, he would complain about how ungrateful I am for not thanking him and saying that he will never do it again but where was my "thank you" for all I did! His demands were illogical and very immature. He wasn't bothered to help, didn't want to help and clearly thought he had no part in the running of the household. I had very little support from him. I thought we were a team but clearly we were not.

His money was his and in his own words "if you don't ask then I won't know what you need." I was surprised by the fact that he did not know bills needed to be paid or food had to be provided. I couldn't understand his way of thinking, I really couldn't! How do you live with someone and yet expect that person to ask you for money to buy or pay for the essentials you also use and need? I was baffled and maybe out of pride didn't want to ask. Though he occasionally gave me some money, most of it was for himself and I used my money to pay for everything.

Over the months that followed my miscarriage, I can recall the many times he had put his hands on me because he didn't hold on to his promise and it happened again and again; and I was expected to forgive him because I am a Christian but also because he apologised. If he didn't get his own way his hands would end up on me for one reason or another. He was a bully. I missed some days of work because my body was in so much pain and aching all over. His slaps would be so hard that my neck and jaw would hurt for days and I would be hearing that buzzing noise in my ears for a couple of days at least. There was no reasoning with him, it was his way or no way. For him, as long as I didn't end up in hospital then it wasn't domestic violence/abuse. I was constantly walking on eggshells when he was around.

This kind of abuse
One thing I use to hate after he put his hands on me was that most of the time he wanted to have sex as his way of apologising but that wasn't what

I needed or wanted. He would somehow force himself on me even when I vehemently objected. I used to lay there wishing to disappear. His breath on my neck, his kisses, his rough hands on my skin, nothing about him at that moment aroused me but rather made me sick, he made me sick. I hated it. Satisfied, he would fall asleep like a baby and I would lay there feeling so dirty. I hated that feeling. There was never a time to discuss what happened. To him sex was us making up. He was completely deluded.

One day I confronted him and said that non-consensual sex is rape, he got really angry with me for saying that. I didn't like the thought of that and couldn't stop to think that my boyfriend was raping me, it sounded so wrong and I was disgusted. "Your body is mine", he said. How can you beat someone and then have sex knowing that the person clearly doesn't want that!? He had no respect for me and my feelings. I dare to say I was like his toy.

He was as demanding as a newborn child. He was a bully and I grew scared of him and what he did and could do to me. Now you'll ask me "Why didn't you end the relationship?" and my answer to you would be that this was not our life 24/7, we had some good moments/days and I was hanging on to my memories of those good moments and the hope that he would eventually change. At that time, I was more focused on making him happy than being happy myself. My daughter and him were my priority in a very unhealthy way. I also didn't want people to judge me, I felt like I had something to prove. I now know I was just scared of the unknown and had very low self-esteem and he knew it.

The fact that we were so up and down all the time didn't help me to gather my thoughts and steady my emotions. I would try to speak to him about my feelings and he would pretend to care but the empathy was never there. Our conversations were mostly about him and the things he liked.

Pregnant again!
In January 2012, I got pregnant again and he was over the moon and so was I because we went through a good couple of weeks before that. The doctor had advised us to keep on trying after the miscarriage to eliminate the chances of another miscarriage. I'm not sure if this is medically proven but we took his word for it.

I remember being at work and calling him after I had done a pregnancy test which was positive. "My girlfriend is pregnant!", he told a passerby. He was very excited.

Because of the miscarriage, I was very anxious at the beginning of the pregnancy so I bought all sorts of electronic gadgets to listen the baby's heart making sure that I was on top of everything. I was also followed up closely at the hospital having regular ultrasound and blood tests but also because I, apparently, have one rather blood disorder which is only developed during pregnancy called gestational thrombocytopenia.[19] The doctor explained that because of this condition, I would not be able to bring my pregnancies to full term and will deliver small weight babies. That was the first time I heard about this condition.

In February, to my surprise, he told me he was going to live in Birmingham. I had never heard of Birmingham until then. He managed to convince

---

[19] **Gestational (incidental) thrombocytopenia** is a condition that commonly affects pregnant women. Thrombocytopenia is defined as the drop in platelet count from the normal range of 150,000 –400,000 / µL to a count lower than 150,000 / µLThrombocytopenia affects approximately 7-10% of pregnant women.

me that there were more job opportunities there. I found it odd but who was I to question him. He wasn't asking me; he was telling me. I really had no say, his mind was made up. He packed up a few of his stuff and left. Our relationship wasn't over so he would come to London almost every weekend. I still wasn't sure what work he was doing there as he didn't want to discuss whatever he was up to so I started becoming suspicious.

What you allow will continue

"Why buy the cow when you can get the milk for free?" is an old saying but is still valid nowadays. For me, it was very natural to take care of him and show him how good of a wife I could be but I gave away too much too soon. A relationship should be 100/100, with each person giving 100%, however ours was very imbalanced - at best 20/80. I was busy giving husband benefits to my boyfriend.

In March, while cleaning the house, I found a micro SD chip on the floor, as I was not sure if it was mine or not, I put it in a reader and connected it to the laptop. Let me tell you that what I saw on that micro SD card was definitely not what I was expecting. The micro card contained pictures of him and a girl half naked posing together, as lovers would, in front of a mirror and a few pictures of the girl posing by herself. It made me sick but what made me come out of myself was the fact that it was at his mum's house! This was scandalous. We were fine at that time so I couldn't understand how and when this had happened. The pictures date stamp was from the beginning of February. I wanted him to know that I knew so I selected one of the pictures and put it as the laptop screensaver because I knew he would go on the laptop as soon as he got home to play Football Manager like he did every night.

That evening when he got home, I was already in bed and as predicted he logged onto the laptop and saw the picture. Maybe I shouldn't have done that but in the heat of the moment I didn't know what else to do because he would have never mentioned this to me. As expected, he didn't say anything, he didn't even apologise in the morning but was more concerned by the fact that I had gone through his stuff even though I tried to explain to him that I didn't. "Why am I being blamed for him cheating?", I thought. He really knew how to twist a situation around and make me doubt myself.

That same morning, he asked to see my phone, again I have nothing to hide so I gave it to him, even put the password in before he could ask. I could see he was searching around for something, going from one app to the other but I wasn't worried. Suddenly, he started shouting at me about a message he found on my Facebook Messenger that I sent a male friend of mine a couple of months after we started our relationship. The message was dated back to 2010 (remember this is now in March 2012) and had nothing romantic in nature in it. He knew the guy I sent the message to but before I could finish explaining why I had given this guy my number at the time, I received a heavy slap across the face. I leapt from the bed in shock. He kept shouting which did not give a chance to explain. That day, I regretted allowing myself to get pregnant again by such a vile and wicked man. I cried like a baby while considering having an abortion. I just had enough of feeling like a doormat. I felt so powerless. He didn't love me.

When I gathered my thoughts, I repented of the thought of having an abortion, it was a foolish thought and that wasn't something I was prepared to do. I clearly had enough and didn't know what to do or who to turn to. My situation was so delicate and I felt ashamed most of the time to share it with anyone. Again, he apologised and explained that he had slept with the girl on that one occasion. He went on to say that it was a mistake which he will never do again. I'm not sure if it was the hormones or desperation but I believed him. I feared being alone and felt like I needed him but looking back I was alone anyway because though he was physically present, I was alone in every way.

We stayed together despite the fact that he was living between London and Birmingham and I somehow really enjoyed it that way, my daughter also did enjoy those weeks. We had our space back, we were able to relax.

One weekend he came back down for a couple of days instead of the 2 days because I had the ultrasound which would reveal the sex of the baby. He was excited but on the day, as we were walking to the hospital, we were chatting and something he said didn't add up so I started doubting what he was up to in Birmingham. I questioned him and there, on the road, we ended up having an argument. He turned around and left me to attend the appointment alone. We had come by car and he had the car key but he still chose to leave me there not knowing how I would get home. All this because he didn't want to answer a simple question about what he was up to over there. He went there for work but there was no evidence or proceeds from the supposed work. I started buying things for the baby with no contribution from him so I had to right to know where his money was going. This was his first child and maybe I was wrong in expecting him to be buying out the whole of Oxford Street.

Back at the hospital, I found out that I was expecting a boy. I walked from the hospital to my house that morning. knowing that I had to get to work. I thought I'd go home to take back my car key as I knew he would then be out and about and I actually didn't expect him to be home but he was. I opened the front door, grabbed my key and left for work. I didn't hear from him that afternoon and only shared the news with him that evening. He was very happy to find out that it was a boy and got name picking straight away. He was looking at his football players list and we agreed on one name. I agreed on the name for what it meant rather than which football player it was. The meaning was very significant for me. I like meaningful names.

Early in April, out of the blue, he decided to move back to London and life as I knew it started again. We were certainly not as excited as he was. I didn't get any time off work when I was pregnant so not having him around was bliss for me. I didn't have to cook certain foods, I didn't have to clean up after him, my daughter could watch tv in peace, I wasn't woken up by loud music and so on. When he was around, we felt restricted because he took over everything, if anything my hormones made it difficult for me to even think straight around him.

Mid April 2012, I was about 4 months pregnant. He was back to his old tricks. He had taken my car for the 3 days and I didn't hear from him until he walked back in the house one morning. This was not the first time he disappeared with my car as he had done that previously for a month in April 2011 only for me to find out that he had shacked up with another girl in East London.

Despite his many disappearing acts, he would still expect me to treat him like a king so he could reap the intimate, emotional, and sexual benefits while also keeping an eye out for prospects who he deemed superior.

Anyway, on Tuesday 10th April 2012 (I remember the date because it is one day before my mum's death anniversary), I woke up to the sound of his keys in the door. He got in bed and I got up to get ready for work. I also got my daughter ready as I needed to drop her to my sister's for the day. I gently nudged him to ask for my car keys. He ignored me. I asked him many times as I was getting late for work but he kept ignoring me. Now, I'm not sure what his problem was but I wasn't prepared to deal with his childish behaviour or leave my daughter with him. I got really annoyed by his attitude and removed the duvet off him. This went on for a while before he pounced up, grabbed me by the throat and pinned me against the storage door in the corridor across the room.

My daughter stood there frightened as she witnessed yet again one of his many violent outbursts. I was thinking "Hold on, I'm pregnant here". He didn't seem to care and ordered me to leave my daughter and go to work. He was shouting in my face and still holding my throat.

The rage in his eyes really scared me. When he finally let go, I made the decision to call the police as he calmly walked back to the bedroom and got back to bed. The police were on their way so I called his mum to let her know what was happening.

The police arrived a few minutes later. I went to see where he was before opening the front door. As I entered my bedroom, I could see he was packing some of his stuff and when he saw me he grabbed me and kneed me in my stomach. I quickly ran to the front door to open it as I thought he may do something else.

One policeman interrogated him in the bedroom while a policewoman took a statement from me in the living room. I couldn't bear looking at my daughter. I was in shock. Even though this was not the first time he had put his hands on me, I told the police it was. All I wanted was for him to be out of my place and he was taken into custody.

An ambulance was called. They ran the basic checks and took me to the hospital for further checks. I had no one to look after my daughter so she came along with me. At the hospital, though the baby had stopped moving for a while, which was unusual, I was reassured that everything was fine after having an ultrasound scan and released to go home.

The police contacted me as soon as he was released on bail which was 24 hours after his arrest. The day after, after much back and forth talk, I stupidly forgave him. I had convinced myself that it was for the best. he did have to appear in court and despite the fact that I didn't want to press charges, the police did.

Little did I know, the hospital and the police had contacted Social Services after this incident. Because of the gravity of the attack, my daughter and unborn son were placed under Child Protection.

When Social Services got in touch I was very fearful as my only reference to their organisation was that they can take children away from their family so I was reluctant to cooperate. I remember being asked "Do you think you will get back with him?" and my answer was "Only God knows", which as a good Christian seemed like the right answer; an answer the social worker was very displeased with as it lacked consideration of the wellbeing of my children. From then on, our assigned social worker visited us at home on a weekly basis, which became rather annoying but after a few visits I decided to cooperate.

Despite being advised we couldn't live under the same roof until the matter was resolved, we still did and things went back to how they were before. Though we had agreed that he would not move back straight away as we clearly needed time apart, he moved back within a week and I feel like I wasn't strong enough to stop that from happening. He quickly made himself very comfortable with his feet under the table, there was no reminding him of what was previously agreed. He had me under his thumb, again. I had to be referred for counselling sessions as I thought it would be good to help me process certain things, emotions and maybe help me make a decision regarding our relationship. As part of his bail conditions, he did have to attend an anger management course and report to his probation officer on a weekly basis.

It took just under a year for social services to close the case. They were satisfied with the process made. We had learned what to do and say at our meetings. The social worker's visits became less frequent. I am not sure I was ready for her to step down if I'm honest. I wanted to tell her everything I was going through but I was very scared that they would take my children away that I kept quiet. I was looking for someone to save me.

The depth of deception
We were living in such a level of deception that even bad seemed good. Things were not great and were clearly toxic. He was still emotionally unavailable, doing what pleased him and there I was trying to please him as best as I could but it was never enough. It was a very toxic environment to live in.

One morning in June 2012, I can't recall the reason for yet another petty argument, he blurred out in anger that he actually got another girl pregnant. It admitted it was the girl from the pictures I had previously found. Yes, she got pregnant around the same time as me (we gave birth a couple of weeks apart). I was beside myself. To make matters worse, I later on found out that when he went to live in Birmingham it was to be there for her as he said. So it was okay for him to leave me pregnant and play house with some else I guess! I was in pieces and to make sure that the knife was fully in, he started comparing me to her because apparently she was the real deal, and she was expecting a girl! He used to complain that my daughter wasn't a "daddy's girl" but then again he never bonded properly with her and was never consistent for her to feel secure.

Of course, he lied to her that he was single and when his lies were exposed he went as far as telling her that he was only with me because I was pregnant. I was deeply hurt. "This was not the life I was meant to live!" I thought to myself. When he had finished insulting me and putting me down, he realised how hurtful he had been and though he said he didn't mean any of it, he still said and thought about it. Later on to make it up to me, he swore that it was a "mistake" that he "loves" me, can you imagine! How could I be so stupid!

He now had 2 babies on the way and no real job, this was ridiculous! He wasn't even able to provide for one household, how was he going to provide for 2? This all seemed like a nightmare I wished to be woken up from. He had cheated on me before so it was only a matter of time before he got someone pregnant I guess.

Then one day Facebook some things were exposed about this girl and was the talk of one of the Congolese well known gossip pages. He got home that day in one of his foul moods and started questioning me about that. The only reason I knew about it was because I got called about it. The Congolese community is big and small at the same time so some people I knew did know who she was and what had happened. He was adamant that it was my doing as if I had nothing better to do between my full time work, taking care of a 5 year old, taking care of my house, taking care of a man child and being exhausted from my pregnancy!

It was late when he got home that evening and I wanted to get to bed but he kept me up as he wanted to discuss the post content and as usual wanted me to make him food. He wouldn't let me talk but yet wanted me to prove my innocence. We were going back and forth and to me he wasn't making any sense. I had no care for the girl though I felt sorry for her but nothing that would make me do what he was accusing me of. I walked back to the bedroom where he had gone in order to bring him the pizza I had made, which was straight out of the oven. I was certainly not prepared for what came next as he quickly took the pizza off the plate and slammed it on my face. Yes, he put an oven hot pizza on my face. I stood there looking and feeling stupid. For a second, I didn't actually realise what had happened. I knew not to scream because my daughter was sleeping next door so I ran to the bathroom to wash my face with cold water and saw that I was scorched on my nose and my eyelid. It was horrible! I couldn't believe it! I stared at myself in the mirror and started crying then I sat down on the edge of the bathtub and cried some more. Many thoughts rushed through my head but I started praying instead and got myself together. It was very late but I decided to go for a long walk to clear my head. When I got back home, I refused to sleep in the same bed as him so I went to sleep with my daughter. I couldn't understand his desire to remain in this relationship if not to torture me. I had the same question for myself as I let him get away with it. It was all mind games really. From his actions that evening, I knew that his relationship with that girl was not over and it was not a one off, though strongly he denied it.

Despite the many things he had done, I still found an excuse for his behaviour and felt sorry for him "poor him, he had got another woman pregnant and kept it to himself. That must have been such a heavy weight on his heart and mind. Poor him. No wonder why he snapped." I think most of the time, I got really good at finding / giving him the right excuses which then made me feel sorry for him even more. Was this not the right thing to do as a Christian? Is that not what you do for the one you love? I then had it in my mind that I should not be so hard on him and try to be more understanding instead.

On the run

At the end of July 2012, I started my maternity leave so I was at home most of the time. I had found him a job in Hamleys which he seemed to enjoy and that meant he got to get out of the house and I had a bit of breathing space.

One morning he woke me up to get to work and asked me to drive him there. He only needed to take one bus to get to work from the house. I had just started my maternity leave so I had a lot of sleep to catch up on and I was simply exhausted. He didn't care and dragged me out of bed "You can always go back to sleep when you come back" he kept saying but that wasn't the point. He rushed my daughter to get ready but I was taking my time to get ready so he got angry. I just didn't want to drive to central London when there was a bus right outside to take him there! I had a pair of scissors in my hand (not sure what I was cutting) and as he was getting more and more frustrated he started asking me for the scissors. I thought to myself "If he takes those scissors I have to make sure I stab him first before he does anything to me", my mind was playing all sorts of scenarios. As he got angrier and started shouting at me, my heart started racing uncontrollably and I became very anxious at the thought that something was going to happen. I really didn't know why he wanted those scissors but my hands and mind were not allowing me to even consider giving them to him. Although I would have never had the courage or intention to stab him, this is something that could happen because I really didn't know what he wanted to do with those scissors.

I was frightened and whispered to my daughter to put her shoes on, and wait by the front door as he had already got her dressed. As he walked towards me, he snatched the scissors of my hand but I wasn't going to wait and see what was about to happen so in a panic I ran to the front door, grabbed my daughter, my keys and ran out of the door. We ran out of the door as fast as we could. I was in my pyjamas and slippers but I ran. Seconds later, I heard him shout my name as he ran after us and believe me I had never ran so fast down stairs in my life, and bear in mind I was heavily pregnant. I knew the lift would take too long so we took the stairs and I could hear him behind us. I stopped looking back and ran up the road holding on to my daughter as tight as I could, the poor little girl didn't know what was going on. We entered our local corner shop and I asked them if I could hide there. They hid us in their basement for what seemed like an eternity and were kind enough to give us something to eat and drink.

The shopkeeper was very concerned and kept looking outside as he could see him pacing up and down the road looking for us. When the coast became clear, the shopkeeper escorted us out and we ran to my car and drove off to my house.

Though we didn't speak much that day, m
sensed that there was something wrong but she
didn't want to push. She welcomed us and gave
me some spare clothes to change into. I had no
bag, only my phone and my keys. I turned my
phone off as soon as I got to her place. I felt very
stupid as I replayed in my head what happened
that morning. I had enough to live like that, to live
in fear of "what next" and for my daughter to
witness all this.

Eventually after a couple of days, we went back to
our house. I was still very distressed by what had
happened but also what I was going to find at
home. I had to go home because I didn't want to
give him the satisfaction of driving us out of our
home. We got indoors that evening and he was
there like "a king in his castle". As usual, he
ignored us for the next couple of days, yes even
my daughter, and I didn't have the courage to ask
him to leave. I thought if I made him as
uncomfortable as possible, he would leave but
that didn't work at all. I stopped cooking, cleaning
his clothes etc. but he couldn't care less.

He also had this thing when he stopped talking to
me and made my daughter serve him food or
speak to me through her. The poor child didn't
know where to stand with him. So much
manipulation in this form of mental and emotional
abuse, it's unbelievable.

After that, you can imagine that the abuse didn't
stop there because what you allow will continue.
Looking back, I realise that I had a very low self-
esteem and allowed his words to have power over
me. I was crushed and thought I was getting what
I deserved. "Was this my punishment for having
sex outside of marriage?" I thought at the time

when in reality I had lowered my values, principles and standards in fear of being alone.

Mixed priorities

The weekend our son was born, that Saturday morning, I was washing the plates but felt "something" odd. It wasn't contractions or anything like that but I asked him to take me to the hospital. I didn't finish washing the plates and got ready for him to take me to the hospital there and then because I knew he had a birthday to go to outside London that afternoon so I wouldn't have the car.

When we got to the hospital, a few tests were done and I was hooked on the monitor which indicated that I was having contractions every 5 minutes though I wasn't feeling them and could only see them on the graph. The nurse kept asking "can't you feel it now? Here it is...There! There! Can't you feel it!?". She was very surprised by the fact that I wasn't feeling anything. She then told me that by the looks of things I would be giving birth that weekend for sure because my contractions were very regular. We made arrangements for my daughter to go to his mum's. Now, as time passed, he seemed to be in a hurry to leave to go to his party though any man having their first child would have dropped any plans that day to make sure they did not miss a thing, he didn't. He did his bit, was reassured by what the nurses had said and left. After he dropped off my daughter and got to his destination, I did not hear from him again.

On Sunday 9th September, the doctor told me, after their morning examination, that I would definitely be giving birth that day so I called him. He said he would be on his way soon but didn't sound like he was in a rush to get back to London.

His journey back took forever! I kept calling him because I didn't want him to miss the birth of his son and honestly I didn't want to do it alone again. Little did I know, he had taken a girl with him to that party and from what I heard they were pretty cosy and seemed to be having a good time. So my understanding was that he had picked her up that Saturday after leaving me at the hospital and dropping my daughter. He certainly took his time to take her home that day. Mind you, I only found that out a couple of weeks after giving birth so this was not addressed until later. The guy who was doing his birthday was a friend of ours who later on told me what happened that day as he thought I didn't deserve to be treated like that. I questioned his motive for divulging this information to me after the event. I asked him why he had allowed him in with another girl knowing that we were together, though I'm not sure what I was expecting him to answer. What made it worse for me, and more sickening, was the fact that he had welcomed his son into this world just after cheating and wearing the same clothes which probably had the girls sent mixed with his own. He tried to deny it when confronted but I had too much proof so he ended up admitting it. I was appalled once again by his lack of care. He made many poor choices but this one had to be in his top 3.

When our son was born that Sunday evening as predicted, the birth was easy. He made it right on time to accompany me to the delivery room. It was a matter of 3 to 4 pushes and the baby was out. The nurses didn't even have time to fully prepare.

The birth of a child should be a joyful moment, a happy moment to share between partners and family but for me the only joy shared was between my babies and me. With my daughter, it was short lived because I was then at risk of losing my life.

With my son, though his dad was present, he made me feel more alone after passing a careless comment not even 1 hour after I had given birth. Though his comment was immature, it still hurt "Wow! You're still big!", he exclaimed. This wasn't said in a nice way at all as he made me feel fat even when I wasn't pregnant and after that too by commenting on my weight, the way I looked and requesting that I started attending the gym, which would according to him would help me look "better". What was meant to be a happy moment became a very awkward and sad moment.

His negative opinion of me did affect me and became my truth.

The illusion of a new beginning

After being discharged from the hospital, I really thought it was a new beginning for us and that things would change for the better because things had been quiet for a while. I thought that being a dad might even change him, which was wishful thinking. I even managed to put at the back of my mind the fact that there was another girl expecting his child. He didn't seem to be in touch with the girl so I just assumed that he had ended things with her like he kept saying. I did tell him that he'll have to take his responsibilities and this didn't mean that they had to be in a relationship. At that point, I had to focus on a newborn, a 5 year old and myself.

About two weeks after I had given birth, his other baby mother gave birth and things turned sour again. I remember it was a Wednesday and we were out enjoying ourselves as a family when he got a call and his mood changed. Even though he told me that they were not together, I still encouraged him to be there for his child so I didn't mind him going to see his newborn daughter.

Children are innocent in their parents' business and should not be used as pawns.

The following day, he told me that he was going to get a train or coach to Coventry to see his newborn daughter. I was ok with that and was actually happy for him to be discussing this with me. He went out to check his account and came back in a foul mood. He then forcefully started asking for my car key but I needed it having a 5 year old and a newborn. I explained that to him but he got angry and started threatening to hit me. I couldn't argue anymore, especially not in the presence of the baby so I reluctantly gave him the car key. He was meant to go and come back that day, but he was gone for 4 days without getting in touch. All I had access to was his changing profile pictures on BBM[20] where he would put pictures of his daughter. When he came back, it was like nothing happened. He was very excited and very proud to show me the pictures he had taken with his daughter. Though I wasn't against him spending time with his daughter but this felt like he was rubbing it in my face. I even wondered where he slept while he was there but deep down I knew the answer.

No one is safe
One day as he was holding our son in his arm (one arm), I could hear him playing football in the living room with my daughter as I was in the bedroom. The living room wasn't that big and I don't think many people would allow their children, or any adults, to play football in such places so I felt like I had to intervene as I could hear the ball bouncing on every wall. I got there and kindly asked him to stop but he ignored me. This is the sort of thing he would do, ignore me which I understood later one is a form of abuse.

[20] Blackberry Messenger.

Because my daughter could see that he was still playing, she continued playing with him and disregarded my instructions. From there, and many other instances, I could see why parents have to be on the same side of the "law" when it comes to raising children as we were sending her mixed messages and she clearly would side with him out of fear. As I stood there clearly talking to myself, the ball came my way so I caught it. He looked at me and firmly asked that I give it back "Give me the ball", he said. Again, I explained to me that as an adult he should be setting a better example for my daughter.

Before I could finish what I had to say, he head butted me and I fell back onto the sofa. My little sister, who had come to visit from France, heard the commotion, ran quickly to the living room and witnessed the end of the scene. She was very angry so she grabbed him by the collar of his t-shirt, "Fils de pute! Connard! Batard! Non mais t'es fou!?", she was shouting and cursing him in French. I was curled up on the sofa holding my head in pain. She said she heard me scream though I didn't hear myself scream as all I could hear was my newborn baby's piercing cry. Our son was crying and screaming at the top of his little lungs, still in his arm, but he couldn't care less. I asked my sister to let go of him because the baby was clearly distressed. She was ready to fight with him. My daughter had backed herself into a corner witnessing this shocking scene. My little sister looked at me with tears in her eyes, then reluctantly she let go of him and took my daughter to the bedroom with her.

The thought that my son could have been dropped at any moment made me sick to my stomach. He was over a month old and very tiny. I was in pieces. I had never been head butted before and it hurt so much, my eyes started watering.

After I gathered myself, I could see he was sitting on the other sofa trying to settle the baby. I didn't know what to do so I went to my bedroom though I knew I needed to get my son off him because he was still crying in distress. I asked my daughter to quietly put her shoes on. I got a small bag ready with essentials, told my sister to get ready as I was collecting my strength to go back to the living room to ask him to hand the baby over. I pretended that the baby needed his feed so without looking at me, he handed him to me. As soon as I got hold of him, we all ran out of the house. I felt stupid but I didn't know what else I could do, I just wanted to get out of there.

After 10/15 minutes of us leaving, he started calling my phone but I didn't want to speak to him so I turned it off. He knew what he had done and I didn't want to hear his pathetic excuses because it was never his fault you see I was always the one provoking him as far as he was concerned.

We drove to my big sister who lived very close at the time. Even though I didn't want to tell her much, my little sister did. Both of them were now very angry and my big sister asked me to drive her to my flat. I reluctantly did though deep down I wanted her to sort him out. My head was pounding and my left eye was swollen, sore and watery. They got into my flat as I waited cowardly in the car. They wanted to fight with him but out of respect for me decided otherwise. It was now a matter of having a serious and firm discussion with him. When they got inside the flat, they found him in the living room, watching tv, looking very chilled. My big sister daringly stood in front of him demanding that he leave my flat. As she was talking, he gave her sarcastic looks but refused to talk. Because she was getting aggravated by his rudeness, my little took her walked her back to the car. "Grrr I hate him!", she angrily let out, as she opened the car door.

That evening when I turned my phone on, I saw that he had called many times and he called again as I was holding the phone so I nervously picked up. He was very calm and as usual apologised and asked where I was so he could come to apologise face to face. I told him he would also need to apologise to my daughter for putting her through this. After a lot of talking, I told him where we were and he turned up the next day. I was very anxious at the thought of seeing him after the incident but I knew it had to be done. We walked around the area and talked. I didn't want him to touch, hug or kiss me. I was ready to break up with him and told him that his behaviour indicated that he was still in a relationship with his other baby mother. That situation was bringing so much stress in his life and consciously or unconsciously he was releasing that stress on me/us. Once again, he swore they were not together and that he was only helping her with their daughter. I felt really sorry for him Even though I wasn't 100% sure that he was being truthful and even though I really wanted to be out of that relationship, guess what? I went back home with him that day which infuriated my sisters and eventually led to more abuse. I was a shadow of myself, scared of the man I was living with.

I've come to understand that you set the standard for the way people treat you and I've learned this lesson the hard way. I had never set boundaries and I was paying the price for this.

One too many break up
Emotional abuse is very subtle and the way some people do it is very sneaky. He broke up with me countless times then always found the right words to say to get back in and I allowed it. He never

had a valid reason to break up but it somehow gave him some sort of "power" and the more power I gave him the more powerless I felt.

In December 2012, which was our son's first Christmas, he broke up with me for a reason I'm still unsure about. He had suddenly stopped talking to me (nothing unusual as I got used to that) but had asked me to drop him at his mum's as I was going out. Because I was going in the opposite direction, I refused. As we got out of the house, he followed us to the car and got in despite the fact that I had said no. I was now forced to drop him as he would not get out. That evening after dropping him off, he called me and broke up with me, that's how much respect he had for me. A couple of days later, he had the audacity to invite us to his mum's for Christmas where his other baby mother would be as he wanted to spend Christmas with his children, he said. This whole situation was a joke to him. I was baffled and rejected the offer. To me, it made absolutely no sense for me to sit there and be made to look like a fool once again. I tried to explain my reasons to him though I knew he would not understand. At first he seemed unhappy but then he got over it very quickly as his baby mother and daughter were staying over with him at his mum's.

He moved back to his mum's that December and my suspicions were confirmed. He was still messing with his babymama. He wanted to make a fool out of me by having us both under the same roof, I was furious. This man was clearly playing us both and as far as I was concerned she was welcome to him. I felt like a weight was lifted off my shoulders.

All he did that Christmas Holiday was being spiteful in his status updates and changing his profile pictures every 2 minutes as he knew I would see how he was playing "happy family" with this girl. It was the Christmas season and I was busy taking care of my children, and to be honest we were doing very well without him.

By January 2013, I think he started realising that I was mentally moving on. My conversations with him were centered around the children and I would not allow him to talk to me about anything else. His way of interrogating made me feel uncomfortable so I had to cut the conversation short. I wasn't interested in his big words and flirtatious ways. The reality was that he was at his mum's with this girl and they were living their life and I got on with mine.

Early February 2013, which I can only imagine was when the girl left, he asked to take me out swearing that he was not with the girl anymore, that she was too immature and he needed a woman like me (whatever that meant to him). He kept saying that it was a mistake. "She is a kid", he repeatedly said. All he was saying was said in hope to convince me that he had come to his senses. It took some effort and a lot of persuasion but I eventually accepted his invitation to dinner on Valentine's day. He made big gestures that day and the plans he had for us sounded amazing at the time. We did have a good time that evening though it was awkward at first as it was the first time for him to take me out. After that, we were back together but he knew he had to regain my trust. I thought having spent some time without him and having enjoyed that time, that I would have had the strength to not take him back but I did. He promised that he would not move in until things were better between us. He knew what to say and I wanted to believe him.

I didn't want him to move back with us because we were fine not having him around as much, and I did think we needed time and space. You can imagine that it didn't take very long until he had his feet under the table. He didn't give me a chance to think properly whether I really wanted this or not.

We went on for a while just being ok as he tried what he called "his best" but it was the same old, same old for me. There were no more fireworks for me, not a single spark. I was putting on a brave face but I realised that I had completely fallen out of love with him. I became very aware that every single touch from him made me uncomfortable. It made me cringe. I was physically there but my mind was somewhere else, too much had gone on and I had put up with too much. My self-preservation mode kicked in.

The help
While going through this mixture of emotions, I confided in my big sister about what I was going through. On more than one occasion, she had turned up at my house to confront him but he couldn't care less because the person who was living with him wasn't strong enough to stand up to him in that same way. She even managed to break my front door on one occasion after I had told her how he had locked me in the bedroom and beat me with his belt. I was ashamed of the whole situation.

Though I sought help from my big sister, I was very annoyed at what she did that day and stopped talking to her for a while as he had convinced me that she had gone too far and disrespected him. I hid myself from the people who cared about me and even found excuses for my good friend to not come over because he felt like she disrespected him after a heated conversation they had. I isolated myself so no one would know what I was going through.

On another occasion, I felt like a naughty teenager as he confiscated my phone because I was having a conversation with a male friend and he didn't like it. He took my phone away from me and hid it for a couple of weeks. I had no choice but to buy another small phone, order a replacement sim card and hid that phone from him until it pleased him to give my phone back.

One last chance

In 2015, my doctor diagnosed me with depression. I was depressed and I didn't know it, though deep down I was feeling really low. I suffered from severe anxiety especially when he was around as I felt like things could kick off at any time. My heart would race uncontrollably at times especially when he would start yelling at me.

I started losing my hair in clumps and developed a type of eczema caused by stress. My body was covered in black patches, except my face. I would also wake up every morning with pains in my hands as I slept with my hands in fists. My body was shutting down and my doctor was concerned. He suggested counselling but I was unsure about it as I had already attended counselling in the past and I was not sure how effective it had been since I was still finding myself in that same predicament.

In December 2015, he once again hit me even though my cousin was in the other room. He had hit me before that of course, but that was the time I had the courage to speak up. With his hand around my throat, I managed to calmly say to him "it's over". By the tone of my voice, he understood that I was serious. He let go of me and took a step back to look at my face. I looked at him and firmly repeated what I had said because I meant it. My heart was racing as I was expecting him to carry on with his assault with more anger as there was an awkward silence before he started pleading with me to give him a last chance. As far as I was concerned, I had given him one too many chances and he didn't make good use of them. Of course, he used his usual tactics to guilt trip me because he knew I wanted the children to have a "proper family" as I didn't get to experience that. Though deep down I knew the children would be better off without him, I thought I was doing them a favour by agreeing to give him a last chance, "This is your very last chance," I said. My answer was emotionless and certainly not what I wished I had said. I wanted out of that toxic relationship.

The beginning of the end

The start of 2016 was very quiet even though I knew it wouldn't last for long. I definitely had no feelings for him. I knew there was no way I could love him again and forget all he had done. Not even two months into the year, I perceived that he didn't change his ways, he just got better at not getting caught. He was making some effort, according to him, but I couldn't see a future with him anymore.

The fact that he didn't put his hands on me didn't change who he was as a man. He had his wicked and twisted ways. I had lost respect for him as a man and as a partner. Despite the many talks we had about the weight of bills and other things that needed to be taken care of around the house, he was still not contributing to the household bills, the rent, inconsistent in providing for food, helping around etc. those were the things that also lacked in that relationship, there was no partnership. I was doing it all by myself. His favourite argument was "If you need money, ask. If you don't ask then you have enough for it all." Utter nonsense! His money was his and he would rightfully spend it on himself. We were both adults but it felt like I had a 3rd child around most of the time.

His life was planned around himself and no one else, which was a red flag I refused to see in the beginning. He was not ready to be a man or a father. He wanted to play the field and I was ready to settle down which I thought had nothing to do with his age but maturity. He travelled mostly with his friends. His weekends were planned around his friends and having fun. I was in a relationship and he was single. No matter how many times we had this conversation, it fell on deaf ears.

Towards the summer, he had made a new female friend which I did not have the pleasure to meet. She had appeared out of nowhere and he called her his best friend. I was not surprised as this was just like him, new friends popping out of nowhere but this one was different. I became suspicious when I found receipts of restaurants and cinema trips in his pockets while emptying them to wash his clothes. According to him, I had nothing to worry about. "Heard it all before," I said to myself. She would come pick him up outside our building in the evening and they'll be gone for hours. Since he was spending so much time with her, I asked to meet her as she seemed to have become a very important part of his life but he insisted it was nothing. To be honest, I really wanted him to be cheating so that would have been a good excuse for me to end things. I wasn't hurt, I was just looking for a way out.

It has to end here
At the end of July 2016, after he failed to turn up on time at my uncle's engagement party, we got home and he started getting ready to go out again. I wasn't aware that he was going out but since my cousin was in London that weekend I gathered they had made their own plans. They had become very good friends after my cousin

had stayed with us for a couple of months in the past. My cousin had made his way to North London by bus where they were going to meet up that evening. I wasn't bothered by the fact that he was going out, what bothered me was his whole attitude that day and that evening.

As he was getting ready, he demanded that I hand him my car key. This was one of the subjects that would 9 times out of 10 create an argument and turn physical. I didn't want to give him my car keys so he became very rude and abusive, nothing unusual. He kept asking and I stood my ground. I now had this new found strength in me screaming, "Whatever happens, girl, do not let him win this time." It was like I knew I had reached my breaking point; I was ready for anything. I had years of abuse from him under my belt and this was the last drop for me, I knew it and I felt it. Because he wasn't taking no for an answer and felt like him raising his voice would get me to give in like he was used to, I hid my car key and firmly responded "No" to his demand. I wasn't prepared to change my mind. the more I said no the more empowered I felt, I was standing my ground for the first time.

I carried on doing what I was doing. I was emotionally detached and ready to take that step. So when he asked for the car key one last time but more aggressively and I gave him the same answer, we got into an argument. "Know your place" he scoffed in the middle of the argument. I sarcastically repeated what he said "know your place! Ha! You must be kidding me, right! Do you know your place?". I reminded him of the many things he wasn't doing as a man and also the time when he asked my daughter who is the king of the house to which she answered "Mummy, because she does everything". After hearing those words, he flew into a rage, truth does hurt as they say. Remember, I had previously told him that if he ever put his hands on me again we'll be over for good, so as bad as this may sound this was the right opportunity as I knew what was coming next.

We were not arguing in the same room as I was in the living room and he kept going back and forth between the living room, the bedroom and the bathroom. I was playing on the floor with our son in the living room when he aggressively walked into the living room and grabbed me by the throat from where I was. My body was forcefully pushed back against the balcony glass door where the handle of the door dug in my back. This time, I didn't look away but daringly stared into his eyes. He shouted abuse in my face then let go of me. The children were looking in shock at the scene unfolding in front of them. As he was leaving the living room, our son asked him "why are you doing this daddy?" and he boldly replied "because mummy is naughty." My son looked at me with so much sadness in his eyes and at that moment I knew this had to end.

That evening as he went out, without the car, I packed a bag with enough clothes for a week and went to my dad's. I was proud of myself but still felt very anxious so I wanted to be out of the house to not have to deal with him the following morning. On the way to my dad's, I thought of many things but the bottom line was that I couldn't keep what I was going through to myself anymore. The first person I shared my ordeals with was my stepmum who was very shocked by it all. She had heard rumours of many things but never confronted me but to be honest I would have probably denied everything. His mum and my stepmum had a friend in common and information went round between friends. I fought back tears as I explained my misery. No one expected this to be happening behind closed doors. They knew he wasn't right for me but not in that way.

My brothers, especially the older one, were very angry to the point where they wanted to gather their friends to go and sort him out. I was against the idea though I thought it would have been a good lesson for him but revenge is never the best option as far as I am concerned.

During the week we were away from home, he kept calling me, messaging me, emailing me and even got his mum to call me but I was on my decision to end things. His mum understood my point. Him and I did exchange a few messages where I made it clear that we were over and that I wanted him out of my house but he wasn't having it. Not only he wasn't getting my point but one minute his messages were nice and he wanted to make up, the next he was being very nasty and abusive. As the abuse kept coming, I blocked his number.

He was refusing to leave my house and said that he would not leave until I came home and had a chat with him face to face. It felt like a set up and I wasn't going to be fooled again. I felt like I was being chased out of my house and it didn't make sense. My cousin was arriving from France and I needed to be home. It was ridiculous! He was being so unreasonable and vindictive.

I picked up my cousin in Victoria station and explained the situation as she was expecting us to go to my house. We stayed one night at my dad's but the next day it was time for us to go home after much debating. He had no rights so I contacted the police on our way home to ask if they could help in removing him.

When we arrived in the area, I parked at the back of my building and they met us there. I knew he was still there as the lights we one. The police, accompanied by my cousin, went to my house but as he refused to open the door so they couldn't do anything. I was very scared to go myself which would have probably been better. That evening we all went to sleep at my good friend's studio nearby. The next day, my cousin and I woke up very early and hid next to my building then took the lift to the floor above mine and waited for him to go to work. We saw him leaving and waited a bit before going inside the flat. I then called my landlord who sent a locksmith to change the locks. My landlord had been made aware of the situation by the police so the locksmith came within the hour. I was happy to finally be in my flat as we were travelling to Portugal the following week and we had to prepare ourselves.

Because my cousin was going to Portugal with us, having her at home made me feel safer and I managed to relax a bit though I feared bumping into him. After a couple of days, I messaged him to come and get his belongings as I had put them all in boxes and left them on the shared balcony which he would have had access to since he didn't give me the fob back to gain entrance to the building and balcony. He got back to me shortly after receiving my message and asked that we meet. I felt stronger so I agreed. Our meeting was very brief and unproductive as he kept trying to convince me to get back with me.

For a while, I couldn't talk to him because his way of thinking was not very logical so there was absolutely no point in trying to have a mature conversation. All I wanted was for him to get his things on the balcony and for us to agree on childcare arrangements.

After this incident, social services were once again contacted to assess the situation because of the concerns raised by the police. Note that when you have minors in the property, it is their duty and obligation to contact social services. From there, social services became involved in our daily lives with meetings at home and keeping tabs with the school and health services such as our GP[21]. As part of their ongoing investigation, the police asked to speak to the children on their own. Though I wasn't comfortable with that, refusing would have made matters worse. During their interview, both children had mentioned their dad had hit them on a couple of occasions. I was questioned over the allegations and they also contacted him. He was quite annoyed and of course blamed it on me. I guess he expected the children to lie or for me to tell them to lie. I didn't deny it not only because it was true but also because I wasn't going to call my children liars when they were not.

A wake up call
Before leaving for Portugal, things had calmed down a bit and when we returned from our holiday, he and I eventually met a few times to discuss how we could co-parent effectively. He would constantly want to talk about us as a couple, asking for another chance, often trying to kiss me or hold me in a romantic way. To be honest, the thought of us getting back together did cross my mind but I was aware that I had to break free from the toxicity of that relationship.

I was focusing on my children and the fact that I didn't want them growing up thinking that "this" is love. For my daughter to think that if a man beats you and abuses you, it means he loves you; and for my son to think that if you love someone putting your hands on them is how you show love. I needed to escape this vicious cycle for their sake and my own. They had already gone

---

[21] a doctor based in the community who treats patients with minor or chronic illnesses and refers those with serious conditions to a hospital.

through a lot. My daughter had wiped my tears countless times and my son had become very scared when he heard his dad raise his voice in the house to the point where he would run from wherever he was to come and see if I was ok. My daughter seemed to know when things would escalate and would take her brother to go to their bedroom until the coast was clear. I saw all that, I saw the worry, the sadness and the fear in their eyes too many times. We were damaging their childhood. We were not happy. He bluntly refused to take responsibility for anything he did to the children and to me, to me this showed me that he wasn't going to change.

He claimed to love me and at first of course I believed him because I loved him too and I wanted him to love me; but telling a woman you love her while hurting her and breaking her heart is emotional and psychological abuse. "A man in love doesn't have to be convinced to love."[22] I had spent most of our relationship trying to convince him that I was worth loving.

I still cannot believe that I let this man abuse me for that long. I lacked confidence and he preyed on that. He made sure to keep me at my lowest by adding fuel to my insecurities and made me believe that no one would ever love me or want me, not only for who I am but also because I now had 2 children and was over 30. I believed everything he said to the point where I doubted my future, my beauty, my sanity, my worth, my strength but no more.

His presence would change the entire atmosphere in our happy home. His mood swings were something I had never experienced or seen before if not in movies. I soon came to realise that I wasn't living, I was surviving. Nothing was worth

---

[22] Instagram quote by @ijennifermarie

that much fighting. My children and I deserved better, so much better. I was ashamed of myself for allowing this to carry on for so long and this is part of the reason why I kept silent and didn't let people know what I was going through. I also felt that he needed to be protected, but from what? When he had made me a laughing stock out there every time he had a chance to cheat with X, Y and Z in private and in public, especially when being around people who knew we were together. "How can a grown woman like me be terrorised by someone she loves?" I thought so many times. I lived in fear, my children lived in fear which made me feel hopeless and helpless. He picked on me and took pleasure in doing so. He created arguments just for the sake of it and to give him an excuse to walk out and do what he wanted to do for a while. He enjoyed controlling us.

Ladies, let me tell you that a man who doesn't value your heart and can easily leave you to entertain someone else isn't the right man for you. He had no problem walking away and coming back. He clearly knew what to say to make me fall back for him and I had convinced myself that without him I was nothing.

Being a victim
I believe God had given me many opportunities to escape that toxic relationship but I was too blinded to see them.

The first time someone told me that I was the victim of domestic violence/abuse, I didn't want to hear it. "Me! A victim? Never!" I thought. I even laughed it off so it wouldn't sink in. I felt like saying "Nope, that's not me, I'm a strong woman". I didn't want to face the truth though I was in every way abused and a victim but I felt uncomfortable hearing those words. It's not easy at all to look at yourself in the mirror, see the bruises (the visible and the invisible) and think you'll be ok. Seeing the man you love constantly mistreating you. He tortured me morally, physically and emotionally. This relationship was doomed from the beginning but I went against my gut feeling and ran towards those red flags. I was blinded by my own desire to be loved and find happiness. Of course there are worse case scenarios, not to be compared, but this, to me, is my worse. "Never again" I whispered to myself.

A few people didn't believe that we would be over for good, so they were very surprised and pleased that I stood my ground. No man is worth that much heartache and headache. I am stronger now than I have ever been, not only for myself but more importantly for my children. It wasn't easy because at times I thought it would be better to just go back with him but that was my fear of the unknown creeping up. It took some time to get over my fears and insecurities but also time to stop messing with him as the flesh was still very attached. I had to set boundaries which was something he wasn't used to. There was a stronghold and I had to break the soul tie[23]. As a Christian, I strongly believe in godly and ungodly soul ties which have positive or negative effects on our lives.

Taking responsibility
In sharing my story, I also take my own part of responsibility in the fact that I chose to stay with him despite everything he did. I allowed him to treat me that way by lowering my standards. I've learned a very painful but life changing lesson in this process which can be resumed but this sentence "You never know how strong you are until being strong is your only choice."

---

[23] A soul tie is like a linkage in the soul realm between two people. It links their souls together, which can bring forth both beneficial results or negative results. Soul ties can also be found in close strong or close friendships.

There is certainly more I could share on this subject and the abuse he subjected me to because, believe it or not, much more happened. I went from being ashamed to being able to openly discuss what I have been through with anyone who asks because this is not an isolated case. I truly believed that I had to deal with it all on my own when in fact together we are much stronger. If you ever find yourself, or know someone in this predicament, know or let them know that they are not alone. Your life matters, maybe not to your abuser but it does to the one who gave it to you in the first place, God. Break the silence, shame the abuser. Talking is one part of the healing process.

Those mind games

I was beginning to heal and come to terms with the fact that I was once again a single mum but this time with 2 children. I tried co-parenting as best as I could but it was just not feasible as it was like he made it his mission to keep on hurting me. He still wanted to control me by any means.

What we agreed was that he would pick up the children every other weekend which started well. Then to be spiteful, he came up with excuses to not pick up my daughter on those weekends. She was a child and couldn't understand what was happening as he would come and get her brother. To annoy me even more, he would turn up at any time on Friday evening and drop him back at any time on Sunday evening. He wouldn't pick up his phone to let me know when he was running late and just turned up. He would bring our son, who was 4 at the time, after 9pm on Sunday knowing that he had to go to the Nursery the next day.

On one occasion, he brought him home around midnight and as he handed him to me casually said "he hasn't eaten and he needs a shower". I was livid. It felt like he was doing everything he could to get back at me and I didn't know how to deal with him because he was not open to any mature and rational conversation.

Again his moods were varied when he picked up his son as one weekend he'll be all nice to me and the next he would stand at the door cursing me in front of the children. This was emotionally draining for me. Therefore, in order to protect my new found peace, I told him that he was not allowed in my house anymore, that he would pick up his son at the door to minimise the abuse. At first, it was a challenge as he thought I was joking but I stood my ground and he had no other choice but to play by my rules which was unusual for him.

Remember a lack of boundaries invites a lack of respect. I needed to respect myself and he needed to respect me. In setting boundaries, I felt empowered. I finally had control over something.

Children's heart break too

During our relationship, he had made comments about my daughter's father, though he didn't know him, but he thought he was better at being a dad than him. Occasionally when we argued, he would say to me "Go look for your daughter's dad." Well, it's not like I didn't have his number or knew where he was but rather that I respected his choice to not be in her life. I found his comments very immature and heartless. To be honest, I'd rather an absent father than one who damages the child by his inconsistency and bad behaviour.

When our relationship was over, he made that comment again as he distanced himself from her who only knew him as her dad. "Enough!" I thought to myself, my daughter deserves better so I was determined to tell her the truth one afternoon. I felt like it was about time she knew the truth because he was playing with her emotions as well as mine. Most of the time she just felt like he didn't love her and that feeling was increased when his focus shifted from her to our son. "I wish I had a different dad" she said one day.

Though I know I should have had that conversation with her earlier on, I didn't have the courage to. I was worried about the kind of questions she would ask and what she would think of me.

I sat her down one evening while her brother was with his dad, as I thought it was the perfect time for us to have that conversation. I must admit I was very nervous but I knew it had to be done. To my surprise, she didn't have many questions to ask about her dad so I thought I'll give her the full story minus the hurtful details. I owed her the truth and at 10 years old she was mature enough to understand what I was sharing which she took it in very well. I didn't speak ill of her father but stated the facts. "Can I see my dad one day?" she asked. Though I had no news from him, I knew how to find him so I replied "I'll see what I can do." I also noted that she wanted to ascertain whether or not her brother was her "true" brother and was relieved by my answer. She hinted that she "sort of" knew that her brother's dad wasn't hers, "It's ok mummy" she said. We hugged and spent the evening watching a movie.

After that, as a courtesy, I told my ex that I had to tell her. He got really upset about it but I reminded him of the many digs[24] and comments he had made and the fact that she deserved better. He had also been abusing her emotionally and mentally by calling her names such as "fat" and by doing the same mind games he did with me i.e. ignoring her when she talked to him if he was

---

[24] a sarcastic remark.

upset with her or me. He lowered her self-esteem and she lived in fear of who he was when he would not get his way. She grew scared of him too. Not only did I have to protect myself but defend her too. He could be so heartless with her. He once called her fat and made her do sit ups by force, she was only 9. My poor baby girl. They were in the living room and I could hear her cry from my bedroom so I ran out as I didn't know what was happening and when he heard me coming he closed the door on my face so I had to push my way in. "Leave her alone" I firmly insisted as I stood between him and her. I knew he wanted to hit me but I couldn't care less. She was defenceless and he was bullying her like he was bullying me.

As our son was growing up, I could also see that he was picking up on some of his dad's behaviour so I had to be very careful. He was quite rough playing with our son and would slap him if he even dared to cry or ask him to stop. All this taught him was to not respect people's boundaries, to be rough/violent and to hit when he was not getting his way. This all became very apparent when he started nursery as the teachers started noticing it and I had to attend meetings in relation to his behaviour. I was very upset about this because I had told him that this would happen but do you think he listened? To him everything I said was utter nonsense and I never seemed to know what I was talking about until he could finally see the consequences and say "You were right, you know." but by then it was too late. We all had to comply with his selfish behaviour or else. "What am I doing to my children?" I thought.

Masquerade
In November 2017, he seemed to have come to terms with the way things though he would still bring up the subject of me and him getting back together. "What would you say if I ask you to

marry me?" he blurred out during a telephone conversation. I didn't want to hurt his feelings but I had to be honest with him so I answered, "You know exactly what my answer would be. I would say no because you've put me through a lot, I haven't got any more feelings for you and I don't believe you are the man God has for me." I had come to understand who he was but also that I deserved so much better. I was now aware of the kind of man I wanted in my life, the kind of man who would also be a positive role model to my children and future children if any.

The week we had that conversation, we talked on Wednesday, he had to pick up our son on Friday. As he stood by the door, he asked if I would allow him in as he needed to speak to me. I really didn't want to. "Please, it's important." he insisted, so I let him in because it sounded like something I had to hear. He was calm and collected though the look in his eyes made me feel uncomfortable. My good friend, who had come to live with us, was in the living room so I felt safe. he didn't want to talk in the hallway so we went to talk in my bedroom which was right in front of the entrance door. "What is it?" I rushed him "What do you want to say that's so important?" I didn't want him to stay too long inside my house for some reason. When he shut the bedroom door, I felt very uncomfortable. "Sit down", he calmly said.

I proceeded to sit on my bed but far from where he was standing. There was an awkward silence as he took him a couple of minutes to gather his thoughts. To my surprise, he kneeled down and took a box out of his pocket. I instantly knew what it was but I kept thinking "I hope it's a joke!". "Will you marry me?" he mumbled while opening the box. The ring was absolutely beautiful but I somehow felt disrespected by his gesture as if my words meant nothing to him. I was angered even more by the fact that he was still trying to wriggle his way back into my life. I looked at the ring and even though it was all I ever wanted in the past, I suddenly wasn't that desperate; and I certainly didn't want it to be him. From our many conversations in the past, he knew I wanted to get married and I may have sounded desperate because I was. Marriage had become an idol and to keep my hopes up he would often promise that he would marry me someday. I did hope he would despite what we were going through but I was completely delusional. I fantasised and romanticised marriage without knowing what it really was at the time. I thought I was ready but the reality confirmed otherwise.

Looking at him, I got very annoyed as he dared to ask the question a few times. I explained to him the many reasons for my decision. After a couple of minutes, he stood up as he could hear my tone of voice had changed and saw that I was getting aggravated by the whole situation. I stood up to get out of the bedroom when I noticed that his mood had changed. He put his arm out to block me from opening the door, I stepped back, "Please let me out," I said. I knew he was hurt but what was I supposed to do! I suddenly felt trapped in my own bedroom and my heart started racing uncontrollably. I asked again that he let me out. He wasn't moving and his arm was still in my way. "Just stay here please," he mumbled "You can come out when we leave." This whole situation and his request didn't make sense to me but I complied though I still came out to say goodbye to our son. When they left, I sat on my bed and replayed in my head what had happened as it felt like a bad dream.

Actions have consequences

That Sunday, he brought our son back from his weekend with him. As usual, he brought him home very late and bizarrely he wouldn't settle to sleep and kept whining. After what seemed like an hour, he still wasn't sleeping and seemed quite distressed so I sat next to him and he said "I don't want to go to daddy anymore." I was surprised and asked "Didn't you have fun with daddy?" "No", he answered sounding quite crossed. Then he went on to explain that his dad had slapped him very hard across the face because he could not close their front door. I was appalled by his behaviour and saddened by how my 4 year old boy was left feeling after that episode which I had no trouble picturing.

Knowing that social services were still involved in our lives made me even more upset because this could be a reason for them to place the child under child protection again.

I texted him the next day as I was very disappointed by what had happened and the fact that I had a very upset little boy to calm down the night before. He didn't respond to my text and I wasn't expecting him to but he did call in the evening. When he called, I picked up the phone and heard him say in a rude manner, "Pass me my son", my answer to that was "Hello!" but he hung up the phone. He called again and started the same way so I greeted him again but this time he replied "You are dead to me". I was taken aback and didn't want to hear what else he had to say so I passed the phone to our son. Once again, he was being very immature and I wasn't prepared to lower myself down to his level. He weakly apologised to his son and made all sorts of promises then got off the phone.

The very next day, we had a planned social services visit at home and as usual they would speak to the children on their own before speaking to me. "Are you aware of what happened to your son last weekend?" she asked. I nodded to confirm I was aware. She asked me to talk her through what my son had told me. After an extensive conversation, she told me that she would need to refer this incident to the Children's Services team in Westminster as he lives in that borough and it was out of her hand.

A couple of days later, I got a call from someone from the Westminster Children's Services team. The social worker I spoke to at the time talked me through the report she had received and advised me to not give him our son until they had spoken to him. She also came to see our son in school to start her own report. I asked the social worker to share that information/advice with him when she would speak to him because I knew all hell would break loose and I would be at the receiving end of his anger.

As the days went on, I became very anxious because I knew that he would not comply and I was right. The social worker called me back that week to say that she had tried to speak to him but he was very rude and put the phone down. "You cannot give him his son until we have completed our assessment," she insisted. She was not impressed by his behaviour at all. I did discuss with her the possibility that he may still turn up at my doorstep, "If he does, call the police and explain the situation," she advised.

The week went on and we didn't hear from him which was great. As the days drew near to the weekend he was to have our son, I became extremely nervous. That Friday, I was very nervous at the thought of what was going to happen as I knew he would turn up. I prayed he would not turn up in school to pick him up which he didn't so we rushed out and I took the children out for some shopping. We got home just before 8pm that evening and the house phone rang around 8.30pm, I knew it was him because his caller ID was displayed. I refused to pick up and put the phone on silent. From the moment he had said that I was "dead to him," I had blocked his number on my mobile and he could only call our landline. He repeatedly called and it became very apparent that he wasn't going to stop so I picked up and passed the phone to our son. "Get ready, I'm coming," he very calmly told him. He couldn't care less what the social worker had said so I texted him with my friend's phone to reiterate what she said. Minutes later, he showed up at my front door. Remember he never gave me my house keys back so even though I changed the lock, he still had the fob that allowed him inside the building up to my front door.

We are all under alert and panicking on the inside. I ordered the children to remain in the living room. At first, he was gently knocking then we heard a loud noise and as he started banging on the door. We all looked at each other and fear started building up, I could see it in my children's eyes and they probably saw it in mine too. He did that a few times then started shouting abuse. I went to the front door and yelled at him to stop as the children were really scared. He stopped for a minute and started again. "I will call the police if you don't leave" I shouted at him through the door. "I don't care, call them," he dared me. Though I didn't want to, I had no choice but to call the police. As well as banging on the door, he would also be calling the house phone nonstop. The children were distressed and started crying. My friend, who was present, was worried about what he would do to me if I dared to open the door. We were all very scared.

I was still on the phone to the police when the loud banging noises stopped so I went back to the front door to tell him that I was on the phone to the police. "I'm calm, Paulette, I'm calm. Open the door." he said but I wasn't going to take that risk so I said "I will open the door once the police get here." Before I could finish my sentence, he started kicking the door again. I could see the door jumping as he kicked it, the hinges were jumping and I could see a bit of the outside. In panic, I put both my hands on the door to stop it from jumping. My friend was in the living room comforting the children but we were at that point all scared of the possibility that the door may break and him getting in. The neighbours had gathered outside and were trying to reason with him but he was clearly having none of it.

The police took a long time to send a patrol car so I called my uncle who lives nearby but he was in south London. We felt helpless. Then all went quiet, the banging and kicking finally ceased. I nervously looked through the doorhole and he was gone. All was very silent, my neighbours had gone back indoors but I was scared to open the door to confirm, so I waited until the police arrived. When they finally arrived, we looked at the door on the outside and all that kicking and banging had damaged it.

The police took my friend's and my statement. They advised me to get a non-molestation order the next day after looking at the whole case as they had access to previous reports and felt like he wasn't going to stop. They could see that the children were distressed. That night, they issued a warrant for his arrest.

My uncle turned up minutes after the police had left to make sure we were all ok. I told him what had happened and he asked me for his and his mum's number as he felt that this should be addressed as soon as possible.

On Monday, I booked an appointment with the family court nearby where the non-molestation order was granted and a copy was sent to the police. As the police had a warrant for his arrest, they went to his mum's house but he wasn't there so that week we were on high alert. It was a very stressful week. I got a phone call from the police one evening, I believe it was on a Saturday, to inform me of his arrest. They were going to give him a copy of the non-molestation order but I suggested that they read it to him before handing it to him. I wanted them to make sure that he had heard the conditions on the order as I doubted he would read it if given to him. They kept him 24hrs in custody and made sure to read the order before releasing him. I was scared he would come back to attack me and became quite paranoid in the street. I had sleepless nights just thinking of the many ways he could get back at me.

Not even 24hrs after his release, I started getting phone calls from a private number then his sister's number. I found that really strange and automatically assumed that it could only be him so I refused to pick up and blocked her number. I got calls many times by a private number, then numbers I didn't know and deep down I knew it was him.

I became fearful and contacted the police but they told me that since it wasn't from his number, and because I wasn't picking up to hear the caller's voice, then they wouldn't be able to prove it was him. A couple of days, he called me but this time with his own number. Because I had blocked his number, it didn't appear as a normal missed call but rather a notification of a blocked caller attempt to call with the time so I reported it to the police. The policeman assigned to the case put me on hold as he said he would try to speak to him about this and ask him to stop because he was in breach of the order. When the policeman got back on the phone to me, he was quite annoyed, "I've had enough of him, "he said "I'm issuing a warrant." The policeman said that he had been very disrespectful. A couple of days later, he was arrested for breaching the order.

The police came to my house to gather evidence on my phone. He was taken in custody and had to stand trial. They kept pushing the trial date as they thought it would be better for our safety for him to remain in custody as he clearly had no respect for the law. The police informed me that I may have to come to the trial to give evidence, the thought of it gave me nightmares and panic attacks. I had to wait a couple of weeks to find out whether or not I would need to appear at the trial. They decided against me testifying because they had all they needed from me and I was relieved. On the day of his trial, he pleaded "not guilty" though the evidence the police had were substantial therefore he was kept in custody. It was his word against theirs. He was brought to court again at the beginning of December 2017 but The judge found him arrogant and his defiant attitude in court was not appreciated. He was sentenced and kept on remand again until early January 2018 when he was released after serving his sentence.

His sentencing was based on his whole attitude and the risk they thought he could potentially be to us. The police also asked the judge to change the non-molestation order to a restraining order which carried more weight. They also advised that my house be placed on a "code red" which meant that as soon as I called the police and gave my address they had to come straight away.

While he was on remand, they managed to get my building fob off him which they were not able to do before. He had told them that my neighbour gave it to him and at first they had no choice but to believe him. Lastly, I was told that I would need to move on emergency as they were not confident that he would abide by the conditions of the restraining order.

During the time he was inside, my neighbour, who he befriended, kept coming to tell me what was happening in court though I did not ask him for any information he may have thought to himself that I wanted to know. To my surprise, my neighbour mentioned that his girlfriend was there, though the last time I checked he was single and proposed to me, so I was baffled. From his description of the girl I knew who she was, it was the girl who he claimed was his "best friend" in the last couple of months of our relationship. I thought I'd be hurt by this new information but I wasn't and that's how I knew I had moved on emotionally. I was completely detached and thought I would tell my neighbour to stop reporting to me.

A very spotty leopard
In January 2018, he had completed his 3 month sentence and was out. When he got out, of course his story was that I got him locked up, that I was the villain but as you have read in the paragraphs above, he had many opportunities to stop all this. Our actions have consequences and we need to take responsibilities but for him passing the blame was always a better option.

I got very annoyed bumping into people we both know who would comment on the situation without knowing the facts and only having heard his version of events. I remember standing in the middle of Sainsbury explaining myself when the following quote came to my mind: "When a toxic person can no longer control you, they will try to control how others see you. This misinformation will feel unfair, but stay above it, trusting that other people will eventually see the truth." That's when I stopped explaining myself to others because I knew the truth and that's all that mattered. He knew the truth too but lying was more convenient. My comfort is in knowing that God will re-establish the truth and expose the lies. I am at peace.

An unexpected message

In March 2018, his girlfriend got in touch with me on social media (Instagram). Her message read as follows "Hey, you probably won't know who I am but I needed to send this message so that I could have a clear conscience. I owe you a huge apology. I've had some negative things to say about you without even knowing you all because of … I'm so sorry because it's only now that I'm understanding everything you did because I experienced similar issues…" I wasn't aware of any of the things she had been saying so her apology was unexpected. Though he may have told her many things about me to make himself look good, I couldn't even understand how a woman would even think that there is any good excuse for a man to beat a woman - there is absolutely no excuse for domestic violence. I wasn't sure if her message was genuine so I thought it would be prudent of me to keep our conversation short. Though I was sorry to hear that she was going through the same issues, I thought it was best to not pass any comment.

A couple of weeks later, I felt like I should message her to check how she was. I don't know the girl but I was thinking about what I had been through and what she may be going through so I wanted to make sure she was okay. When I messaged her, she seemed to be doing well which was good. Then, she started talking about my ex and our son's relationship. What she was saying sounded very much scripted and she had changed her tune from her previous message.

What she didn't seem to understand was that I had never stopped him from seeing our son, I had tried my best to co-parent with him which didn't work then the court order stated that if he wanted access he should apply through the family court and I reiterated that to her. The restraining order was very specific in terms of contact.

From the tone of her messages, I got the sense that they were back together. She did not know me or the life we lived prior to her meeting him but she was adamant that he was a good dad. I'm not sure how she gathered her information but from her seeing him with our son every 2 weeks for 2 days she managed to paint this perfect picture of him as a dad.

We exchanged a few messages but I felt like she was playing the advocate for a man she barely knew. His own family wasn't as concerned as she was. Though I understood what she was trying to do, the way she was trying to sell his good parenting skills to me got me thinking if it was really her sending those messages. Because I doubted the source of those messages, I cut the conversation short, wished her well and blocked her. The bottom line is, if he really wants to see his son, he had been given the steps to follow and from where I stood he was looking for an easy way to go around this. Going to court meant that he would have to pay all sorts of fees and the judge would also be looking at his background and recent sentencing to make a decision which may not have been in his favour. The judge may have given him limited access or he may have to see his son in a contact centre at best which I'm sure isn't what he would want. This would have been once again about me doing him a favour by not going to court but I really want things to be done by the law for him to take responsibility and be accountable.

I didn't report him to the Child Support agency because I haven't got the desire to do that. It may sound foolish but I'm not after his money, all I ever wanted was for him to step up as a father and take care of his son by providing a safe and secure environment for him.

Narcissistic behaviour

I am not a psychologist but from all of the above, it is clear that my ex had many issues which he refused to face or even admit to himself. I have observed him during our time together and came to the conclusion that he is a narcissist who suffers from Narcissistic Personality Disorder. It became apparent to me from examining our relationship and from reading the following definition: "Narcissistic Personality Disorder (NPD) involves a pattern of self-centred, arrogant thinking and behaviour, a lack of empathy and consideration for other people, and an excessive need for admiration. Others often describe people with NPD as selfishly arrogant, manipulative, selfish, patronizing, and demanding." Doesn't that sound just like him?

Chapter 5
A new beginning

After all my ordeals, I eventually but surely woke up to myself thinking "I deserve better", better late than never! I thought about my childhood, my teenage years and all that I had been through and surely this was not the life I was created for, a life of constant pain and heartache.

<u>Brighter days straight ahead</u>
My journey of healing and wholeness began in 2018. After the break up, I focused on getting the children settled and well, I didn't stop to think about myself. One day, I suddenly became aware of my brokenness.

On the 1st January 2018, I remember waiting on God for a word which I knew would set the tone for the year ahead and not only did he give me a word but he gave me two, "obey" and "testimony". Now I wasn't sure what God meant by that but it wasn't long before I found out (see next chapter).

I started the year feeling free mentally but I craved for more freedom, I knew I could tap into more and I wanted more. Being free from my past wasn't enough, there was more freedom coming my way and the challenge was to remain free which isn't often easy.

My memory kept replaying the many things I had been through, not just the abuse and the broken relationships, but also the life choices I made for myself. I consider myself a logical person, though I must admit some of my choices have not been very logical but I tend to question everything and often I would think of different endings for the many situations I faced.

Growing up I had so many dreams, hopes and aspirations but there I was a single mother of two. I felt like a joke, like a failure. I regretted the many choices I had made. I was aware that I wasn't living the life I was purposed for but "Where do I start?", I thought to myself. I wanted to start building my inner strength so I started reading, not any books but inspirational books and drawing closer to God as I must admit that I definitely didn't have a consistent relationship with God at the time. I hadn't read the bible or any books in ages so there I was doing my devotional and reading one book a week. My mind was opened to new things; things I somehow knew but forgot about. I started to feel empowered and I loved it.

At times old habits crept in, those are the things we often do without thinking or realising which become/create our habits whether good or bad, in my case they were bad. I had to change and/or break a few of my old habits. I was aware that some of my habits were birthed out of a painful and broken place. Now that I was feeling a bit more like myself, I needed to birth new/healthy habits out of that happy and peaceful place, a place where I was becoming whole.

Being a single mum
I never thought much about single mothers before becoming one. Though I had many apprehensions about raising a child on my own, there seems to be a social stigma around single mothers which I experienced. Single mothers are often thought of as run down, unkempt, irresponsible, exhausted, selfish etc. Some people would even go as far as thinking that it is our fault if we are single. In fact, most single mothers didn't ask to be one. The trouble is that

many people worldwide in the government and media have a terrible opinion of single mothers.

Being a single mother is not always due to the physical absence of a father but also the complete lack of involvement from that father even when he is around. With that in mind, I had been a single mum throughout my past relationship because he didn't play his part. I was used to taking care of the children by myself! I was in a relationship with someone who made me feel single in every way possible.

Though motherhood came naturally to me, I did find it hard to answer the tricky questions my children often asked about their fathers. Children are so innocent. Although they witnessed the abuse, they still wanted to know if he was ever coming back. They may have not understood everything at the time but they certainly understood the need for a radical change.

The majority of single mothers I know are strong, independent, hardworking, educated, motivated, happy, and fun to be around. Yes, it's challenging but with the right emotional, physical and mental adjustment, it's not impossible. "You make single motherhood look easy," some of my friends commented and nicknamed me "supermum". To be honest, I just do what I've got to do and get on with it. Yes, I work full time, I cook while supervising homework, drive the children to their various activities, serve at church etc. and still have time to socialise regularly but to me this is all part of motherhood, single or not.

After God, my children are my number one priority and I'll do anything for them, within reason.

Raising well balanced children is not as easy as we think but I was set on making sure that despite our shaky beginning my children would still have a chance to make it through this life mentally and emotionally stable. A lot has to be taken into account when raising children, things we never thought about, things we took for granted when we were growing up ourselves. One of them is the fact that raising children with the wrong partner could possibly scar those innocent souls for life. Before we send them out to the big wild world, we are our children's first role models so we ought to take that seriously enough to want them to be and do better.

As a matter of fact, I do believe that without my children, I would have maybe still been in that toxic relationship. My children, without saying a word, helped me make that lifesaving decision. I left that toxic environment because to me it was what was best not only for me but also for them.

My relationship status has nothing to do with my quality of life, I am a mother who happens to be single...for now.

Finding lasting happiness
Until recently, I had always wanted to be happy which I don't think I ever was before. My happiness pretty much depended on those around me who thought I was happy when in reality it was all an act. I wasn't happy with myself, the way I looked and the life I was living. Don't get me wrong, I had happy moments and I was happy being a mum but that was just that, nothing sustainable.

"Never put the key to your happiness in someone else's pocket."[25]

My journey to happiness began when I started decluttering my mind, my life, and my flat. I use the word "journey" to describe the process

---

[25] unknown author.

because I believe happiness is a destination. I knew I had to get rid of the things that weighed me down and the things he had left behind which were a constant reminder of the past. I felt really good doing it!

As the days, weeks and months went on, I was wrapped up by a sense of peace and inner strength I had not experienced before. Though things didn't look perfect at all, I was happy and at peace. I found myself giving importance to the person who mattered the most...me. I neglected myself all these years while putting everyone else's needs before my own. I let myself down trying to please those around me. Things had to change, I had to go back to the source of my happiness...God.

I found happiness when I reconnected with God, friends and the church community. I had to go back to the foundation of my belief i.e. who I am in Christ and who God is. I had neglected my relationship with God because I was consumed with all kinds of negative emotions. I avoided connecting with anyone at church in fear of being judged because I did find some Christians to be more judgemental than the people of the world.

I took time apart to seek and rediscover the God who created me. It was beautiful! My eyes were opened to new and old biblical truths. I absolutely enjoyed, and still enjoy, being in His presence. I missed that. Mind you, He said "I will never leave you nor forsake you"[26] so he had never left my side, I was just too blind to see Him.

Forgiving
Between you and me, I must admit I had to do extensive work on forgiveness. As unbelievable

---

[26] Hebrews 13:5 - Keep your lives free from the love of money and be content with what you have, because God has said, "Never will I leave you; never will I forsake you."

as it sounds, I first had to forgive God. As shocking as it may be, I was angry with God.

In the past, I questioned God a lot as I did not understand why He allowed those horrible things to happen to me/us. I had "lost" faith though I prayed, I was not convinced my prayers were being heard. I felt like God could and should have prevented many things from happening in my life but He didn't. I believed in God but I simply did not believe God could do anything for me. I saw Him work in other people's lives but not in mine. I was hurt, frustrated and angry at Him. I had to verbalise my feelings towards Him in a prayer that started a bit like this "Dear God, I'm angry. Yes, I'm angry" then paused as tears flowed down my cheeks then in the stillness of that moment I heard Him say "It's ok" which made me cry even more. Just like David in Psalm 22, I had to pour my heart out. As I quietly mumbled the words of my prayer, I realised that God didn't need to be forgiven as he is a just God, fair and impartial. Some of what I had been through was simply the consequences of me stepping away from God and seeking my own will and desires. I had to be honest with myself and take responsibility and draw close to Him to be reconciled.

My biggest challenge was forgiving myself. It was hard though I knew God wasn't holding anything against me, I simply couldn't forgive myself. I felt like I had failed God, I was disappointed in myself. I carried around the feelings of shame and guilt. What really helped me was soaking in the truth that I am forgiven, loved and created for a purpose. My head knowledge, theory, had to connect with my heart and be put into practice. I had to let go of what my mind was telling me, all the "could have" and "should have" and see myself through God's eyes.

I struggled to come to terms with God's love. It didn't make sense to me that he loved me despite my many mistakes. "I deserve to be punished" I often thought to myself but this was due to my knowledge of how earthly fathers deal with their children. We do not need to do anything to earn God's love, He chose to love us and nothing can separate us from His love, not even our sins.[27] God isn't anything like our earthly fathers, though there are some similarities, God is a thousand times better. I was limited in my understanding of the fatherhood of God which I constantly compared to the experience I had with my own father. God forgives, He never holds grudges and never brings up our past[28], how wonderful is that!?

I then worked on forgiving those who hurt me, it wasn't easy as we can often justify the need to hold grudges or hold on to the pain as a reminder to never trust again. There in a part in the Lord's prayer[29] that says "...forgive us our trespasses[30] as we forgive those who trespass[31] against us..." as a believer this taught me to extend grace in the same way I received it. Forgiving limits the influence of the person who hurt you, I didn't want to be limited by unforgiveness. One thing I always say is "I will not miss heaven for anyone."

Something we all ask ourselves is "Do I need to forget when I forgive?" Let me start by saying "forgive and forget" is not found in the Bible. However, there are numerous verses

---

[27] Romans 8:38-39 - For I am convinced that neither death nor life, neither angels nor demons, neither the present nor the future, nor any powers, neither height nor depth, nor anything else in all creation, will be able to separate us from the love of God that is in Christ Jesus our Lord.

[28] Psalm 103:12 - He has removed our sins as far from us as the east is from the west.

[29] Matthew 6:9-15

[30] a sin or offence.

[31] to commit an offence against (a person or a set of rules).

commanding us to "forgive one another."[32] As Christians to be unwilling to forgive can hinder our relationship with God and can reap bitterness. To answer the forgetting part, I found my answer in 1 Corinthians 13:5 "Love keeps no record of wrongs." It's easier to love one another when we are not busy keeping records of wrongs, easier said than done but not impossible. After all, we must apply godly wisdom to our relationships/friendships which can help us avoid enduring unnecessary hurt.

Another thing for me was to terms with apologies I never received or thought I deserved. How? By releasing my expectations, the hurt and situations in God's hands. Believe me, I did find peace in doing that.

Nelson Mandela said *"Forgiveness liberates the soul, it removes fear. That's why it's such a powerful weapon."* My take of this wonderful quote is "Forgiveness is liberating. You are stronger when you forgive."

I fasted, meditated and prayed until I felt the release in my heart that allowed the Holy Spirit to move in and change my perspective to God's perspective on things.

Confessing

I mentioned in the previous chapter that I had lied to one of my exes about being pregnant and having an abortion. That had played a lot in my mind as I was going through the process of forgiving. I was thinking of a way to actually get in touch with my ex to come clean. We had met a few times at different parties but I didn't have the courage to do that and it wasn't the right place for sure. Every time I met we met, he would say

---

[32] Ephesians 4:32 - Be kind to one another, tenderhearted, forgiving one another, as God in Christ forgave you.

"Why did you get rid of our child?" then he would ask "Are you sure your daughter isn't mine? How sure are you? Can we do a paternity test?" I really had to put things straight and tell him the truth. At the last party we met, I asked for his number and pondered on what the best way would be to tell him.

In August 2018 while on holiday in Bulgaria, he called me after we had exchanged a few messages. In the middle of the conversation he asked "Were you really pregnant with my child?" I saw this as one of those God moments to come clean so I told him everything. "I'm really sorry, can you forgive me?" I said, "I do," he said "But are you sure your daughter isn't mine?". He was very convinced that my daughter could be his but there was no way he could be her father. "I would have been very happy if she was yours, believe me" I said, because he is a great father to all his children even though he is not with their mothers, he takes care of all 4 of them and I knew he would have taken good care of my daughter and she would have been happy to have him as her dad.

Maturing in my faith

While going through my times of trials, I was still attending church and I would cry uncontrollably during worship time while lifting up my hands to a God who seemed so far away. I couldn't make sense of the depth of my brokenness. "Jesus died for me, for us so where was the power of the cross in my life" I wailed. I felt like God was completely out of reach. I was deeply hurt and felt like God didn't care about me.

One of the books I read during my season of healing was "Wholeness" by Toure Roberts and it was an eye opener. This book is filled with so much wisdom to bring one to wholeness. I learned that my identity in Christ is what will bring me to wholeness, not any man, not material things or any earthly pursuits. This book deals with your past hurt so if you are seeking healing, I strongly recommend it. My brokenness had nothing to do with God but everything to do with my sins and being away from my creator, maybe not in the physical but on the inside.

I realised I had to change my focus from my circumstances to the Maker of all things that's when it all started to change, that's when strength started building up on the inside. I felt like God was putting the pieces of my heart back together but it was a slow process and I needed to be patient. Wholeness is a lifelong journey.

Looking back, I realise that God has always been there with me, I just couldn't see Him through the high walls of my pain. The emotional prison I was living in was one of my own doings as I had consciously refused to see the signs and red flags as I kept going in the wrong direction. I stuck myself in a situationship[33] as if I had a point to prove then couldn't get out of it because of guilt, fear and shame.

Healing

Healing, if not supernatural healing, doesn't happen overnight. I had to be patient and gentle with myself, especially every time I fell or slipped into old unhealthy habits. It's not easy doing it on your own hence why we need God but you have a part to play, you have to want it and be determined to see yourself through the process.

When you are busy doing things to please others, just like I was, people don't get to know the real you. I grew worried at the thought that nobody

---

[33] a relationship that has no label on it[,] like a friendship but more than a friendship but not quite a relationship

would ever like the real me so I pretended to be somebody else. I needed a reboot.

To find yourself after traumatic experiences, you will need to do a lot of painful digging, searching and unravelling but in the end you'll find...you! Be consistent in pushing through.

"You cannot heal in the same environment where you got sick." I had to read this quote more than twice to get to the depth of its meaning. The environment where we seek healing from shouldn't be where we look for healing, that's what I understood.

In the season of searching for myself, God had asked me to be still[34]. I absolutely hated that because it didn't come naturally. Like anyone, I can become impatient, and being still required the patience I didn't have at the time. "Aaargh! God what are you up to?" I was screaming inside but I obeyed. Well, while I was busy moaning about the season I was in, I became aware that the storms raging inside of me had been silenced and I was able to hear God's sweet voice a bit clearer. My feelings towards certain situations had changed overnight. This was a move of God. It may not have been a physical move as such but something had shifted in the spiritual realm. It started with my mind, by casting out all the negative words I had heard over the past years, to my heart which needed a deep cleanse and finally my mouth as I had become very critical of myself and became like a second nature to put myself down.

One big part of my healing process was to cut every unhealthy soul ties and allow God to deal with the desires of my flesh. At first, I felt like a quick prayer would do the trick but I was pressed

---

[34] Psalm 46:10 - Be still, and know that I am God.

to go deeper and wrote down all my past relationships and friendships. I made a list of those I was intimate with and the rest, because soul ties are not just physical. I made sure I didn't miss anyone out then prayed over it and burned it as a symbol that all those unhealthy ties were severed and have no hold on me. It was freeing to watch that paper burn and being blown away by the wind.

Break generational curse

Reflecting through my past, I can point out some similarities in what I had been through, how my life was and what my mum and my grandmother had also been through.[35] I can see the same similarities with my maternal aunts and a few women in my maternal family. When this became apparent, I could see that none had lasting relationships/marriages, violent partners or if in a marriage they had to strive to make things work, nothing was ever easy for any of them. We also seemed to have a curse on our finances - poverty. Also, for example, my grandmother, my mother and all my mother's siblings have had at least one child with a different dad and out of wedlock. I, myself, have 2 children with 2 different dads. Coincidence? No, I call generational curses which were sadly inherited.

To be able to break generational curses, you first need to identify them. Certain types of sin can be passed on from one generation to the next where children are likely to choose to repeat the sins of their fathers such as alcoholism, abuse, fear, emotional instability...

---

[35] Exodus 20:5 - You must not bow down to them or worship them, for I, the LORD your God, am a jealous God who will not tolerate your affection for any other gods. I lay the sins of the parents upon their children; the entire family is affected—even children in the third and fourth generations of those who reject me.

Without the help of the Holy Spirit, it would have been difficult for me to identify those family curses. As painful as it was to see the trail of those curses repeating themselves in my life, I had to ensure that none of it would affect the next generation - my children.

The cure to breaking generational curses is repentance, faith in Christ and a consecrated life to God. "Why am I paying for the sins of people I didn't even know? Why should I repent for the things my mother or my grandmother did?", I thought, because curses don't happen without cause.[36] Somewhere down the line, someone did something against God and this was simply the outcome of it. When someone up your family tree gives spirits the right to visit because of sin, they come looking for a reason to mess up your life. I had to stop it. "It ends with me," I said with a firm voice, taking authority over those sins and situations in prayer.

Generational curses come through our blood line and can only be cancelled by blood, but whose blood? It's all about the blood of Jesus as He was presented as a sacrifice for our sins[37]. I'm in Christ and in Him there is no more condemnation.[38] In Him, I have the assurance that God's grace lasts much longer than His anger.

Generational curses are broken through our faith in the work that Jesus did. I am a generational curse breaker creating new generational blessings for my children and the next generations which last much longer[39].

---

[36] Lamentations 5:7 - Our ancestors sinned and are no more, and we bear their punishment.

[37] Romans 3:23-26

[38] Romans 8:1-2 - So now there is no condemnation for those who belong to Christ Jesus. And because you belong to him, the power of the life-giving Spirit has freed you from the power of sin that leads to death.

The silver lining

As mentioned at the end of the previous chapter, the police had requested that we be urgently moved out of our flat and had contacted the council to make it official. I was placed back on the bidding list with 1,200 points which meant that I will likely move within the year.

Between April and July 2018, I visited a couple of flats. I was even at the top of the list of one that I really wanted but it was scooped away by a family with greater needs, I was devastated. I was then offered a flat but my heart was not at peace. When I went to sign the tenancy agreement, I was very anxious and broke down in tears. I was stressed and felt pressured to accept as I knew I could not refuse it. The way the bidding system varies from one borough to another, in my borough I was only entitled to 2 refusals and this would have been my second, meaning they would have either put me at the bottom of the pile or worse taken those points away. Nevertheless, I had to take a leap of faith and refused the property. I trusted that God had a better one for us and He did. In July, I visited a property which I really liked and as I was the first on the list it was automatically offered to us. The property offered had a garden, 3 bedrooms (we had 2 bedrooms) and they were renovating it which was a bonus. This was God's favour and grace, faith rewarded.

It took a while for the renovation to finish and when they did, I became overwhelmed by what we called the "big move". We had to pack up 11 years of our life in just a week.

By the end of August 2018, we were sort of settled in our new home. Our old place had too

---

[39] Exodus 20:6 - but showing love to a thousand generations of those who love me and keep my commandments.

many bad memories, and just like me the children were glad to see the back of it. It was our new beginning and for real this time.

In all honesty, I was scared of the unknown but I kept hearing at the back of my mind "It's never too late to start again." I had to come to terms with the lessons learned in my past and apply the wisdom gained to better our future. I was not prepared to let my children or myself down again.

As I found myself becoming happier with who I was, my emotions settled and I started seeing everything around me through a different perspective. I came to understand that I had lived a life directed by my own insecurities which affected many of my choices. I had this unknown fear on the inside that rose up every time I was about to make a life changing decision but this time I was strong enough to silence it and make faith filled moves.

God knows my tomorrow so I decided to deal with one day at a time, "to each day its own struggle."[40] I so often tried to overtake God on my journey but this time I was determined to let Him lead and follow His instructions. He has never failed me and He will never fail.

---

[40] Matthew 6:34 - Therefore do not worry about tomorrow, for tomorrow will worry about itself. Each day has enough trouble of its own.

Chapter 6
Walking in purpose, on purpose

In writing my story on paper, I realise that I had been quite disobedient to God. I thought I could succeed without God and convinced myself I could. At times, I even thought that God needed my help in planning and arranging things in my life. Most times, and without saying it out loud, I thought that God was against me and didn't want me to be happy or succeed. But looking back, I could see that I had created my own unhappiness by refusing to follow the path God had laid right in front of me[41]. It was that simple "obedience is better than sacrifice"[42]. I repeat "our choices have consequences!". We basically reap what we sow.

A new revelation
As I sat and reflected on my new found revelation and freedom, I started praying more than I ever prayed before. And as I became more intentional in my pursuit of God, His voice became clearer to me each day.

I'll have to take you back to July 2017 when God specifically told me to start praying for my future husband and enrol in Bible School (IBIOL[43]). At first, I was sceptical but I knew I had to move by

---

[41] Deuteronomy 30:15-20
[42] 1 Samuel 15:22 - But Samuel replied, "What is more pleasing to the LORD: your burnt offerings and sacrifices or your obedience to his voice? Listen! Obedience is better than sacrifice, and submission is better than offering the fat of rams.
[43] International Bible Institute of London.

faith and obey. This was the beginning of many things with God. I had never desired to pray for my future husband and didn't know where to start. I looked up a few things online and started praying some prayer lines I had found which gave me a great insight as to what a godly man should look like. Not only was I praying those prayers for this unknown man but I thought I ought to also be that person too so I prayed the same prayers over my life after all, you attract who you are, right!

Bible School, IBIOL, started at the end of September 2017 but until it started I was still hesitant because of my finances. I had many debts to repay and bills to pay. One evening, God put it into my heart to send a message to my contacts asking for financial support. Again, I was hesitant, those who know me would know that I don't like to ask for help or worse, money. But I had to obey, I sent a broadcast message to my contact list and got no replies for a couple of days. I was very surprised that none of my close friends replied but got two unexpected replies. One of the replies came from a girl I hadn't spoken to in years! They both offered to sponsor my first unit which was more than I expected. This was God's doing, no doubt!

In that same season, the church was recruiting volunteers for the various ministries. I wasn't very keen on volunteering again at church because of my past experience. My daughter wanted to help out in the Children's Ministry so I went along with her to get more information and see what she could do. The young woman at the stand asked if I wanted to join and I shared with her my past experience and told her that I believed it wasn't "my calling". One thing I was interested in was to maybe volunteer as a Sunday administrator because that's something I would surely enjoy. Surprisingly, not to God, they did need help in the Sunday school admin team! I then remembered a word I had read in a book called "25 ways to prepare for marriage other than dating" by Jamal Miller which suggested "while you are waiting, become a waiter" which implies serving in the house of God. I did find what he wrote in his book very inspiring and it resonated with me, especially in the season I was in, "Why not" I thought. I sure wanted to be found serving and making good use of my gifts.

The knowing

When Bible School started, I was very excited and expectant. The first unit we had was "Counselling Level 1" which focused on Christian counselling more than secular counselling. As the unit unfolded so did my purpose. My eyes were opened as to what God wanted to do with me through this not only Bible School but my life. I was slowly being directed into my purpose.

I was very excited about the future and potentially going back into ministry. My mind was filled with great ideas I couldn't contain. I was pressed in my spirit to email the Children's and Youth Pastor offering my services as a "Youth Counsellor". I knew nothing about the youth ministry but the idea of helping the youth through their critical issues in life became very appealing to me. I absolutely loved the unit and the wonderful knowledge I gained which was transferable and applicable. I had no idea what being a youth counsellor entails but I was adamant that this was what God was calling me to be. This was it, I had no doubt about it.

As I typed up my email, I kept thinking "this pastor is going to think that I am a bit bold coming at him like that". I read the email about five times before clicking on the "send" button and I waited, there was no going back, worse comes to worse I would just send an apology email the following week. I mean I just had 3 or 4 lessons on the subject and here I was believing that this was my calling, "You go girl!" I cheered. Well, God never lies so I confidently sent my beautifully worded email and got a reply a few days later. In short, the pastor's reply was "I can confirm that this has been on my mind for the last few months..." I had to do a little praise dance when I read that email because God never fails. He sure knows what He is doing and when He is doing it. I was once again amazed by the way He was paving the way for something great to be done in me and through me.

Going back some years ago, I received a prophecy about the ministry God called me to which I was told would be with the youth. Though I said "Amen", deep down I had rebuked that prophecy and never prayed that it would come to pass. I didn't think I had what it takes to minister to the youth but I feel more spiritually equipped now. It was never in my plans but I had to remember what Isaiah 55 verses 8-9[44] says. Like Jonah, I could no longer run away and hide, it was time to obey what the Lord had said.

The youth pastor called a meeting with another young woman and myself as she also had youth mentoring in mind. I had met the youth pastor at church on a couple of occasions previously, since sending my email, but didn't know the young woman he was referring to. I became very nervous walking up to our meeting venue and had to silence the voices in my head who had me questioning myself "Who do you think you are?"

To my surprise, it was a very relaxed meeting. We introduced ourselves and discussed our heart and vision for the youth ministry and how the

[44] "For my thoughts are not your thoughts, neither are your ways my ways,"declares the Lord."As the heavens are higher than the earth,so are my ways higher than your ways and my thoughts than your thoughts.

mentoring programme would fit into it. To ease us into this new ministry, the pastor asked us to regularly visit the Sunday youth service on, to get to know them and for them to get comfortable having us around. This was at the end of March 2018.

After each visit, I became more and more convinced that I was in the right place to serve. Every interaction with the youth reinforced my desire to work with them. My desire is for them to know God for themselves, to know who they are in Christ and be anchored in that reality, to see Christ manifested in them as the shine for Him and impact those around them, their generation.

A new venture
After a couple of meetings, things were put in place and we were able to start what we called "Life Coaching" which is a 10 weeks one to one mentoring programme. We promoted the programme at the youth service and were able to start mentoring soon after. I was very excited to be a part of something as life changing as this, not just for the youth but also for me.

On one hand, mentoring proved to be challenging at times as I had to make time for it and double my time in prayer, I had to be intentional, more organised and disciplined. I had to research specific topics to gain more knowledge and learn to have a different approach with every youth I mentor as they are all different individuals. On the other hand, mentoring is very rewarding as I saw the girls I mentored maturing throughout our sessions. I believe those 10 weeks are enough for us to plant seeds which will birth good fruits in God's timing. Whether we realise it or not, it does impact their life. Those one to one sessions helped me break out of my shell and as I became more confident, I was able to occasionally lead cell groups and be a guide at some of the youth encounters[45] and even summer camps.

I can attest that my obedience to God has allowed Him to work powerfully in and through my life. Since then, I have seen doors of favour open like never before. This has stretched me in a way I never thought I could be. But all I can hear God say is "This is just the beginning". This is very exciting! I seem to have activated something in my life that no man can stop. God met me where I was and patiently walked me to where I am now.

Sharing my testimony for the first time
In June 2018, I was blessed and honoured to be invited to share my testimony as a domestic violence survivor in Downview Prison which is a prison for women in Surrey, UK. My only reference of prison was in movies and TV series so I was very apprehensive. I had never been inside a prison so my mind was playing all kinds of negative scenarios. I was nervous but excited at the same time.

This was the first time I had to share my testimony in public and I kept thinking "What if they get bored or start laughing at me or even start a fight?". I also didn't know who was part of the group we were going with which made me even more nervous.

In preparing for that day, I was told that I would have to share my testimony in 10-15 minutes "How can I share 6 years experience in 15 minutes?" I thought to myself, but the organiser asked me to focus on what I believed was important for others to know when it comes to domestic violence/abuse. I thought I would prepare bullet points of my testimony which would

---

[45] An encounter, also known as a retreat, is a weekend away with different sessions of worship, teachings and prayer. It is a life changing experience with God.

help me stay on track. It was a crowd of young girls in their early 20s who needed to be able to relate to my story and feel empowered by the end of it like I was.

On the day as I was driving down to the prison (1 hour drive), I was praying on the inside that God would allow me to speak with confidence as I am not a public speaker at all.

When I got there, the organiser met us in the car park. As the young women of the visiting group gathered in the car park, we were directed to the prison's main entrance and talked through the prison visitors' rules. Apart from the organiser, I actually knew a couple of girls so I felt a bit more relaxed. The girls had bought some home cooked food, nibbles, drinks and all sorts of goodies to share with the inmates.

The rules were:
1. Because we were/looked as young as the inmates, we had to wear red bracelets to be identified as visitors.
2. We were told to sit by 2 on each table and they should be no more than 4 inmates per table as they were expecting a lot of them to attend the event, of course the prison guards stayed nearby.

The warden in charge walked us into the prison through secured doors and gates to get us to the room we were using that day, which was the prison's chapel. We were all looking around us as if we were suddenly aware of our surroundings. I somehow felt claustrophobic and overwhelmed by the sensation of being in a big cage. I remember thinking "Wow, I'm in a prison."

When all was set, we gathered to pray and commit the event in God's hands. It was a great fellowship moment.

Shortly after, the inmates were escorted in. The girls looked so young! I couldn't believe it. To my surprise, they were not wearing orange or striped overall like in the movies. Apparently in the young offenders' unit, they are allowed to wear their own clothes hence why the guards needed to be able to tell us apart. They definitely could have easily been mistaken for one of us.

The plan was to engage in conversation to get to know them and their stories. I didn't know what was appropriate to ask so I nervously engaged in a conversation with one of the girls sitting at my table then quickly relaxed as the conversation flowed. I genuinely wanted to know more about her and her story and she responded well to that.

As they were told to help themselves to what we had brought, they rushed towards the big table where most of the food was (sausage rolls, chocolates, chicken wings, crisps and more). One girl even shouted from across the room "Caprisun!" as she ran to grab a couple. To see the smile and joy on their faces was priceless. I felt privileged to be free at that moment and thanked God. "What's happening with...?", they asked all kinds of questions about different things they knew and loved on the outside such as music artists and TV series.

One girl shared with me that she had been arrested because she had hidden a gun for her boyfriend. She had come to terms with the fact that she would be spending a long time in prison. That broke my heart. She was the same age as one of my younger sisters and now she had to spend her best years in prison for a decision she may or may have not made herself. She felt like she had to be loyal to her boyfriend who was also arrested and imprisoned.

After a while of chatting here and there, it was my turn to share my testimony from the front. As I stood up and walked to the pulpit, I somehow wasn't nervous at all. "Why am I not nervous?" I thought as I was expecting to be shaking and stuttering. I mean, this is my story right so obviously not everyone would relate to it and I made my peace with that, maybe that's why I wasn't nervous. I was now standing in front of a crowd of strangers gathering my thoughts.

I looked around the room before starting my testimony and they all looked intrigued as to what I was going to talk about. As I was sharing my testimony, they all seemed very focused and I could see a genuine interest in their eyes, even the wardens. They remained very silent throughout while nodding their heads in agreement to some of my statements. I shared a few words of encouragement at the end which were more or less "Sometimes we make broken choices out of a broken place, because we don't realise how broken we are on the inside. Blah blah blah. You owe it to yourself to be happy, blah blah blah. Asking for help in any situation doesn't make you weak. Blah blah blah. Someone who loves you will never intentionally hurt you or put your life in any danger." And after what seemed like an hour standing up there, I stepped aside encouraged by the sound of their applause as I walked back to my seat. Their applause made me feel stronger and alive, I know it sounds silly but I felt empowered not only by that but also in hearing myself openly share my testimony.

As I sat back at my table, one of the girls from our group came from across the room and asked "Would it be ok with you if we announce at the front that you are available if some girls want to have a chat with you or ask questions," I replied "Sure! Of course! I'd be very happy." She then shared with me that one of the inmates at her table was in tears while listening to my testimony. "Oh wow!" I said, I couldn't believe it, that really moved me. The girls at my table were also full of questions, "You are very strong! Well done for getting rid of him." they commented "I don't know how you managed to even stand and share this with us. Thank you." another one added. I was humbled by their many kind words of encouragement and by the love I could feel around the room. I had to try very hard not to cry because I nearly did because I realised how far I had come. If I'm honest, I didn't see myself as strong as they thought I was but God reminded me that when I am weak, He is strong and He gave me that strength. He made me stronger at the end of it all for His glory.

We played a few fun games, danced, and even had a motivational speaker share an empowering message with them. In the end, we shared our faith with them, ate some more until it was time for us to leave.

I couldn't believe how time flew. The girls didn't want us to leave and to be honest we could have stayed there the whole day. Party bags containing treats such as a diary with motivational words were handed out. There was plenty of food left over but they were not allowed to take any back to their cells. As they scattered to go back to their cells to be accounted for, I could see some girls stuffing their bras with chocolates, juice and other things. As my eyes caught one of them, we looked at each other and laughed. I wasn't going to be the one to report them to the warden, no way! This was "A class" smuggling! "Enjoy it girls!" I felt like shouting.

As the room emptied itself, I stood on one side waving them goodbye. More girls came to talk to me, to express their appreciation of my testimony and to wish me all the best in the future. One girl hugged me tightly as her eyes filled with tears. "I can't believe you have been through all that," she said. Yes, it was unbelievable but yet so true.

These girls taught me a valuable lesson that day: You don't have to look strong to be strong.

As we gathered in the car park once again to say our goodbyes to each other, we were all so grateful and thankful for the experience which we agreed was a success. It was a very humbling experience for us all. I kept my red visitor bracelet as a reminder of my freedom. I will treasure the memories of that day for a very long time.

I realised that we often take our freedom for granted and never stop to truly appreciate what this means. We are living free forgetting those who are fighting for their freedom every day. I am aware that prisons are for criminals but there are also "innocent" people who didn't know any better and were the results of their upbringing and environment. But that's not all, while some of us live in physical prisons, others are in mental prisons. What does freedom mean to you? How do you know you are free? We all want to be free of course but we've got to define freedom[46] accordingly. I lived in a prison of my own for many years as you previously read and although I wasn't in cuffs or chains, it still felt like it. I wasn't free, I was a slave to my fears. As Christians, we understand that our freedom was bought at a great price and have the responsibility to walk in that freedom every day[47]. We have faith that Jesus' work on the cross has set us free from our sins, bondage, slavery, guilt and so much more.

---

[46] the power or right to act, speak, or think as one wants. / the state of not being imprisoned or enslaved.
[47] Galatians 5:1 - It is for freedom that Christ has set us free. Stand firm, then, and do not let yourselves be burdened again by a yoke of slavery.

Keep on sharing

In December 2018, the motivational speaker who attended the event in prison, got in touch with me and asked if I would be able to come and share my testimony at her book launch. She thought that my testimony would be perfect for people to relate to as one of the book chapters is entitled "When a relationship breaks down"[48]. I was honoured that she thought of me though I was anxious to once again stand and speak in front of strangers. I knew what I had to do so without hesitation I seized the opportunity. It was a very beautiful event and indeed the perfect place for me to share my testimony. Once again, the words of encouragement I received that evening were more than what I expected. I was reminded of how strong I am by those who carefully listened to my testimony because apparently, I don't look like what I have been through which to me is a compliment and also a testimony to God's grace over my life.

To me, walking in purpose has and still is what I aspire to do and the way I do it is by obeying God. Some of the things I've had to do made no sense to me or others at first but then like a dark room being subject to the brightest light, it suddenly made sense. He has not called me because I am better than anyone else but he certainly knows what He can do in and through me so I trust Him. Even when I doubt myself, I still trust Him. As human beings, we like to be in control and to know the "why" of everything but don't often know where the answer lies. The idea of living a life without knowing why I am alive, was distressing for me and who would know that answer if not the Maker. In the end, I had to go through what I had to be birthed into my purpose. Rest assured, it doesn't always happen that way. You don't have

---

[48] Life After Death by Vimbai Nashe Chinhoyi.

to suffer to find your purpose but if you run away from God, you have to be prepared for it.

In July 2019, I was blessed to go on a mission trip to Jamaica. That was my first mission trip ever and again I got to share my testimony during a church service. I must admit that the more I share my testimony, the more freedom, power and grace I seem to be walking in. It is not easy to be vulnerable in front of people you know or strangers but this has been an unveiling moment in my life, my history has made me who I am today and I should not be ashamed of it.

This is me
Today, I am more myself than I have ever been. I have chosen to live in the reality of God's love and forgiveness. My love for God flows out of His love for you and because He loves me, I am able to love others with that same quality of love. I'm still getting to know myself a little bit more every day but what I am most happy about is the fact that I can be myself with those around me which is something I struggled with in the past. There is no more pretending. This is me!

In November 2019, I connected with a Christian Mentor on Facebook after she held a webinar[49] called "How to Exude Feminine Energy and Attract Cherished Relationships". She was offering a free online session so I signed up out of curiosity. We started with a casual chat as she wanted to get to know me then she asked a few personal questions about my life (parents, friends and past relationships). I was very surprised by how she was able to bring together all that information and draw clear summary from it. She meticulously analysed my answers and here's what she was able to say about me: "You grew up not having a role model or models of what healthy

---

[49] a seminar conducted over the Internet.

love is, you had no example of healthy relationship/true partnership. Your abandonment issues manifested in a form of not trying to be in a serious relationship. You were afraid of what it is like to be vulnerable. You have been used to relationships going wrong in your life. It has also manifested in people pleasing. Because people have let you down, you have been feeling like you need to do extra to be loved or for people to like you. You continually feel like you have to give. A part of you deep down feels like you have to do a little extra in order to be loved. In relationships, this can lead to you being a pushover. You never communicate your boundaries clearly. You do whatever it takes for people to like you or reject them before you are rejected." I wanted to disagree out of pride but she was right.

I completely agreed with what she said and could see myself doing some of the things she described in my past friendships and relationships. She called this "limited beliefs". I had, and may still have, limited beliefs about myself and the world around me, but I am now willing to acknowledge where I lack and work towards making myself a better woman. I was certainly done with people pleasing after my last relationship. I think my nature is pretty much set in a way that I like doing good for others but I know that it has been taken advantage of many times in the past, but also at times people may have thought that I wasn't genuine. I like seeing and making others happy but I also need to learn to set healthy boundaries around that.

Unhelpful thinking patterns
In the past, my unhelpful thinking patterns stopped me from having healthy relationships (those are the thoughts formed in our heads between the ages of birth and 7 - love, finances, how the world works, etc.), and I realised that God had started to change those beliefs in me.

The fact that I used to be limited in my beliefs meant that I denied myself many opportunities. In my mind I imagined the worse or made certain issues seem bigger than they were which made me feel absolutely miserable. This was a constant battle in my mind which I seemed to be losing most of the time. I wasn't living up to my full potential.

Those unhelpful thoughts were the result of an accumulation of negative emotions but nothing I couldn't change.

In writing this book, I take full responsibility for what happened to me in the past as they were my decisions and consequences. The only reason we should look back; is to see how far we've come. Your journey, like mine, may be a hard one but give yourself some credit as you overcome what was meant to tear you down. Do I regret some of the choices I made? Absolutely! But without those trials, those mistakes, I would not be the woman I am today[50]. No one can bring up my past to break me because it is what made me. The bible says "if God is for me, who can stand against me," that's all I need to know, I am secure in Christ. I know that something greater is ahead of me, I believe it and I have faith that this too shall pass. I am blessed despite what things may look like to the human eye. I am good enough. I am more than enough.

---

[50] Romans 5:3-5 - We can rejoice, too, when we run into problems and trials, for we know that they help us develop endurance. And endurance develops strength of character, and character strengthens our confident hope of salvation. And this hope will not lead to disappointment. For we know how dearly God loves us, because he has given us the Holy Spirit to fill our hearts with his love.

In the past, my smile hid a lot of pain, shame, guilt, fear and so much more that anyone could ever imagine. I looked very composed on the outside but was crumbling down on the inside. I must admit I became very good at faking it. Nowadays when I smile, it is birthed out of genuine happiness, I am content not just in who I am but who I am in Christ. Previously, my identity was in the things of this world, the things I've been through, the things that I allowed to define my worth, hence my many disappointments. I had also given people the power to define me because I didn't know who I was. I chose to put God above everything that concerns me and what you see is the result of my total surrender to Him.

By God's grace, today I have overcome my many battles, most of which were internal and I know it was not by my own strength. Sometimes, you've got to hang on to God as if your life depends on it, because it does.

So often people hide away from what they have been through, allowing their pain and experiences to make them bitter. We don't have to pretend that all these things didn't happen to us, our scars and our story may one day help someone. From my own experience, I know it's very hard to recover from hurt and pain but you have to want it because it is not impossible. There'll be trials, storms, valleys and so much more along the way but you've got to stick to the plan, God's plan[51].

Purposed
"The purpose of every Christian's life is to shine for Christ." - *Andrew Anyanwu, Children's and Youth Pastor, KTLCC.*

---

[51] Jeremiah 29:11 - For I know the plans I have for you," declares the LORD, "plans to prosper you and not to harm you, plans to give you hope and a future.

To live a life without purpose means not having any clear direction/vision for your life. Your purpose is what you were created for and in finding it, you found yourself. God created each and every single one of us with a purpose. He has given us gifts and attributes/characteristics that no one else has. It's like being a piece of a giant puzzle, without you playing your part the puzzle is incomplete.

People most probably expected me to be bitter which would make sense, right! But look at me, I'm winning every day and in every way. I have overcome, I have defied the odds. What was set to destroy me, what sends many into depression and despair has now made it into this book to give hope. I cannot take the glory away from the one who has been with me through it all. I am certain that God has a way of working all things together for our good.[52]

The good news of Jesus, the gospel, is somehow unbelievable because we wouldn't expect a perfect God to love us as imperfect as we are but no matter how we feel about it is true, He cares for us more than we will ever know. When you choose to believe in Him, the impossible becomes possible. I have seen God's hand at work in my life more than I would like to admit, even in my darkest hours, He was there. From now on, I have chosen to live a life of thanksgiving, giving thanks for every blessing I get, the small ones and the big ones.

God has restored me, a broken girl and this is my story. I am unashamed of the things that made me who I am today. I'm done hiding and pretending. I'm certainly not where I want to be in life but I know that God is not done with me yet.

---

[52] Romans 8:28 - And we know that all things work together for good to those who love God, to those who are called according to *His* purpose.

If in reading this book, you were able to relate to some parts of my journey and/or feelings, I pray for a miraculous healing over your life right now. I pray that you will be set free from any form of bondage and that you will find lasting freedom and happiness, not in the fleeting things of this world but in Jesus who never changes. I am a living proof that you are not defined by your past nor by what people think or say about you.

My advice when you see someone struggling with any kind of sin is: extend the same grace you once needed and received.

If you are a Christian believe that in Christ you are made new[53]. If you are not a Christian, I pray that this book, my testimony, will draw you closer to God and that you will want to know Him for yourself and experience the power and freedom that comes with salvation.

Lasting change

Have you ever heard that quote "You glow differently when you're with Christ", or even "You glow differently when you pray."? Well, those are not just quotes they are a reality. Having Christ in my life has had a real impact on the way I see and do things. The real transformation happened on the inside which then overflowed on the outside.

Our problems are generally internal while the manifestations of those problems are external, therefore God deals with us from the inside out to bring lasting change.[54]

---

[53] 2 Corinthians 5:17 - This means that anyone who belongs to Christ has become a new person. The old life is gone; a new life has begun!

[54] Mark 7:15 - Nothing outside a person can defile them by going into them. Rather, it is what comes out of a person that defiles them.

To live in that constant reality, I had, and still have, to surrender my heart to Christ in prayer on a daily basis. Every day, I hunger and thirst for more of God to be manifested in my life and through my life. "I'm not perfect" is no longer an excuse as I have a perfect God living inside of me.[55] Having a relationship with God changes everything, this is better than religion.

Though a smile can hide many pains, it will always be our best asset.

"Just because a person smiles all the time, doesn't mean their life is perfect. That smile is a symbol of hope and strength."[56]

To God be the glory.

---

[55] Romans 8:30 - And those he predestined, he also called; those he called, he also justified; those he justified, he also glorified.
[56] unknown author.

Acknowledgements

Writing this book was harder than I thought and more rewarding than I could have ever imagined. I thank God that as painful as those memories were, I did not feel the pain in the same way I experienced it at the time and that's how I know I am truly healed, I have and I am forgiven and I am on the narrow road that leads to life I was predestined for. None of this would have been possible without God. He has always been loving, faithful, gracious and patient towards me. He deserves all the glory for this life changing testimony and for the many things to come.

A very special thank you to my sister-friend, Abena, who spent time reading early drafts, editing with me, giving me advice and challenging me. You were as important to this book getting done as I was.

To my family. To my mother, Yvette: thank you for teaching me resilience. You always had a great attitude towards life and taught us the value of family. You will never be forgotten. To my father, Garcia: Thank you for being patient with me. I know I wasn't easy on you at first but we are still learning from each other. To my children: I love you more than words can say. My daughter, Yva-Rose, you have seen things I wish you could unsee but you have shown so much strength and gentleness in character throughout these years. My son, Rafael, my little trooper, you have a strong character but yet so caring, loving and kind. To my big sister, Patricia: thank you for being there through the ups and downs. Your presence and love have always been a safe place for me.

To my sister from another mother, Elodie: You have been such a great friend over the years and became an entire part of our family. Thank you for remaining true to yourself at all times.

Many thanks to Pastor Amanda Dye for writing such a beautiful foreword and for your encouraging words.

To the rest of my family and closest friends, thank you for believing in me and for your continued support in this journey called "life". You are all an important part of my life and story.

Lastly, to the friends who encouraged me to write this book, thank you for believing that my story was worth sharing.

This book is the accomplishment of a prophetic word I received in July 2018 by Pastor Emmanuel Apiafi.

Printed in Great Britain
by Amazon

36269050R00106